PURPOSE PATHFINDER

A Personal Development Mastermind on Identity, Self-Mastery, Workplace and Career Fulfilment.

FAITH EHIRA

PURPOSE PATHFINDER
A Personal Development Mastermind on Identity, Self-Mastery, Workplace and Career Fulfilment.

Copyright © 2023 Faith Ehira
faithehira@novarcoaching.co.uk

For information on getting permission for reprints and excerpts, contact the author via:
purposepathfinder@novarcoaching.co.uk

ISBN: 979-839-3242-0-39

Published By:
Nova Results Coaching

CONTENTS

ACKNOWLEDGEMENTS

For the gentle, loving and intentional leading of God each time I ask for clarity on my purpose, for the way He teaches me using His anointed vessels, for the guidance of the Holy Spirit and the grace of Jesus, I first acknowledge My Heavenly Father for this work.

I am thankful for the gift of life, the sacrifice of Jesus for me to be identified with God and the abundance of inspiration the Holy Spirit provided for PURPOSE PATHFINDER. Thank you, Lord, for making my purpose clear to me and giving me the mandate to teach this with clarity.

My beloved husband, David. You support me immensely with the kindest words of encouragement and your actions! My love, I could literally feel the vibes of the actual word 'support' from you. Thank you so much for carrying this vision with the value and importance it deserves and helping me to look further into the future. Thank you for the nights you stayed up to look at my work, and for your corrections and praise for the book. Thank you for cheering me on!

Sharon and Priscilla, my best friends. You are the definition of joy! Thank you for coming into our lives and filling our home with so much laughter and fun; thank you for the daily hugs and kisses and for understanding when Mummy must work. Thank you for being there at every step. You will keep making God proud as you live in purpose daily.

My loving parents, Deacon Jerome and Mrs Mary Olaki, thank you for an excellent upbringing and your constant care; I love that you check up on me so often, so this is an open letter for you to keep doing it. And for your continuous prayers, I see God answering them always and I'm grateful for this. I love you dearly.

To my Spiritual Parents, Revd Olusola and Revd Mrs Oyenike Areogun, thank you for constantly ministering to us the words of life and the true undiluted gospel of Jesus Christ with practical wisdom from the Holy Spirit.

I want to specially appreciate my Visionary Coach, Ministry Gift and Mentor, Pastor Debola Deji-Kurunmi. Your ministrations and teachings have built, blessed, and benefited me greatly. Thank you for being so profoundly awesome. I celebrate the grace of God upon you and I thank you for yielding to the call and raising others powerfully to do the same. You mean so much to me and my family!

My dearest fervent Sister whom God gifted me for mentorship and guidance in the early covid days and who has been instrumental to ensuring this work comes out excellently, Minister Omowumi Toni Falade; keep the fire burning and keep up the good works. Thank you for all you do.

My fervent sister, Opeyemi Odunola, you are beyond amazing! Thank you for your meaningful inputs and wise insights.

My Editor, Chinyere Distinguished Chimezie, you did exceed my expectations. I am glad to have worked with you, love that you are a genuine child of God and a truly wonderful person. I pray that you go higher and do many exploits. Thank you.

To everyone else who has contributed to this work in one way or the other, I am grateful for the gift of you, you are special to me!

FOREWORD

I congratulate Faith Ehira on this stunning work that articulates, in simple yet significant ways, the definite path to a life of purpose and power.

In distilling the Compelling Codes of Identity, Purpose, Giftings, Original Design and Personal Mastery, this amazing author offers us insights and instructions on God's process for preparing, pruning and propelling us into our Divine Destiny.

The contemplations, concepts and convictions shown in this rich resource will offer you a Roadmap for finding, fuelling and fulfilling your God-ordained purpose, while developing your extraordinary talent, unlocking your unique potential and building your leadership capacity, across any sphere of influence. Whether as a young person, student, entrepreneur, career professional or ministry gift; the fundamentals are the same. We all require weighty wisdom to break problematic patterns, install positive paradigms and pursue true transformation; and if all these matter to you, then *Purpose Pathfinder* will give you real results.

I carry a compelling conviction that this book, **PURPOSE PATHFINDER**, will align you with the truth, tools and thinking that you need to shift your life into significance, as you leverage your abilities, build formidable alliances, master your genius, and expand your expertise. Go for gold with your vision and maintain the belief that you're destined for greatness.

May God bless you!

Debola Deji-Kurunmi
Transformational Coach for Visionary Leaders

PRAISE FOR PURPOSE PATHFINDER

I dare say that **PURPOSE PATHFINDER** will take you on a full circle visionary journey of discovering the 'you' God intended at creation. With a detailed exposition on finding identity as a function of the only true origin of mankind, Faith Ehira's personal life story creates a relatable mix as you will see yourself gliding through roadmaps, pausing as you reflect on your purpose journey, and then begin again as you uncover the God deposits within you waiting to be fanned into flames!

PURPOSE PATHFINDER would leave you gasping in awe at the recognition of the divine gifts right within you. With God's love being your focal point, and setting aside all distractions, you will grab a pen and move in action to influence your world one purposeful step at a time.

This book is truly a gift for all, at all ages and stages in life. So, I invite you to take this voyage with the One who knows you best. The true Purpose Pathfinder – God, the Father.

~ Opeyemi Odunola

Author, Just Breathe: Praying Consistently When The Words Don't Seem Enough

As a Workplace Spiritualist who handholds employees in finding meaning, value, and motivation in their work beyond pay checks and performance, I find **PURPOSE PATHFINDER** by Faith Ehira a catalytic tool for life and career advancement.

Faith was able to create a simple, relatable yet powerful context about Purpose. It doesn't matter the grade level of an employee, once they can access this Mastermind, they will receive a succinct Purpose Pathway that will redefine their work-life synchronization.

I would recommend that this book becomes a coaching guide for Human Resource Departments across industries and organizations globally. It's time we started to redefine Employee Training within the context of Purpose and Destiny fulfilment.

~ Omowumi Toni-Falade

Workplace Spiritualist, Organizational Leadership and Employee Performance Coach

PURPOSE PATHFINDER is a timely book that shares practical, step-by-step wisdom to help anyone discover their identity and walk in the fullness of purpose. It sheds light on the concept of identity, in a down-to-earth manner that sets the stage for healing from insecurities or ignorance about who God has made us to be. Building on this foundation, it discusses the topic of purpose, sharing tips about how each person can find and walk in their God-given purpose and make God proud with their lives.

I highly recommend this book to everyone looking to find and live out God's intentions for their lives.

~ **Okezi Obrutu**

Physician, Researcher and Author

Purpose and Purpose Discovery have seemingly become cliches in our world today, watering down their significance and the weighty roles they play in our living fruitful and fulfilled lives in our transient stay here on earth. So, I greatly applaud and deeply appreciate Faith Ehira for this deep and detailed expository on **PURPOSE PATHWAY**.

This book is indeed a mastermind, a rich resource for everyone – young and old, male and female – who desires to live out fully the purpose for which he or she was created. I recommend that parents and teen's coaches/teachers should introduce their kids/wards to this book early and discuss the Purpose Actions in each chapter, so these young ones will not have to struggle with their identity and purpose discovery as most people in my generation do.

Also, I recommend that a physical copy of this book should be in the family library of every home, especially those intentional about raising, moulding and guiding their children in the way that they should go.

~ Chinyere Distinguished Chimezie

Author and Principal Consultant/Editor, Kompendia Concepts

INTRODUCTION

The two greatest gifts anyone can give him or herself is to have a great sense of identity and purpose. Discovery of your identity is the springboard that would launch you into finding and fulfilling your purpose.

In the writing of this precious book, long before I understood the correlation between identity and purpose, one thing I knew for certain was that God would have me start with identity; and He led me on how to go about it. It is important that as you read this book, you pay close attention to each segment. As you do so, you will find the revealed secrets of having a strong sense of identity, understand the in-depth meaning of purpose from different angles, and discover where you currently are – purpose-wise, as well as where you need to be in living out your best life daily.

No matter how many times you have heard this, you have to believe it: we truly are limitless beings! We abound in abilities, we have unlimited strengths and capabilities for expression - both as individuals and especially as a united community of like-minded, goal-oriented people. God sure poured Himself into mankind. Everyone is special and unique, and when you acknowledge this, then you are able to operate at the core of the deposits God has placed inside you, with a full sense of identity and purpose so much so that there's no comparison or competition with anyone except the then, the now and the future versions of yourself.

Purpose Pathfinder, with the well broken-down explanations and examples contained herein, is an empowerment tool that will solidify this knowledge in you and make the application to your personal life an easy possibility.

So, if you are bursting with energy but seeking to understand your unique place of assignment; the knowledge of your niche from exploring the wisdom in this book will give you a cutting edge to extraordinary performance.

Perhaps, you want to come out of certain mentalities that you have hitherto held on to and be baptized into a new revelation, awareness, grace and strategy to be and to do according to the intentions of your Creator who is the only true God, then, I welcome you to a new beginning as you soak in the lessons from this book!

Finally, if you are ready to truly discover how to walk in the depth of your calling with a sense of fulfilment and true satisfaction, you're in the right place - right here and right now! With step-by-step approaches on how to move from purposelessness and dissatisfaction, to understanding your identity, potentials and purpose, this book will empower you with insights to the vision, encounter, calling and revelation you need.

It is an amazing and exciting journey ahead and I am confident that you will get the most out of it.

PREFACE

Like every human who has/had a similar background as mine where I had access to several sermons on purpose, why I must live and leave my footprints in the sands of time, not just exist, I desperately needed to crack the code of how to do this. To have an in-depth understanding of my God-given purpose, I invested quality time in praying and asking God to show me my purpose and what I am here for. I did get answers and I am still getting answers. However, the best response I received from God was the knowing that I would understand my purpose in life as I go through my journey in life. This has been true to my experiences as I can boldly say that God has revealed my purpose to me and guided me through it as I pass through life.

He continues to do this and provides the answers I seek.

The second and equally powerful source of understanding purpose for me would be my teachers, especially as I intentionally pray about this topic and follow great men and women who are already well-grounded in the subject of purpose, that God highlights to me. Teachers like Dr Cindy Trimm, Rev Olusola Areogun, Dr Caroline Leaf, Rev George Adegboye and Visionary Leader Debola Deji-Kurunmi. Their profiles, journeys, achievements and palpable walk with God has birthed in me, and as well, developed and greatly sharpened my understanding of purpose. These success stories with mine as a Life Coach have been great tools for birthing this book, by the divine help of the Holy Spirit.

This book was written with you in mind. Journey with me through the pages of this mastermind and experience for yourself what an in-depth understanding of purpose can do to your overall wellness and spirituality, for your destiny fulfilment in life.

PART ONE
IDENTITY

CHAPTER ONE

AN OVERVIEW OF IDENTITY

"The greatest discovery of life is self-discovery."

At birth, we all came as a total package. No one higher or lesser than another and all without a care. The one thing that differentiates us at the time of birth is the diversities we are born into which includes family, race, tribe, religion and so on.

Identity would never seem to be something of importance to a child until he gets to a point where he begins to have an awareness of himself and the world around him.

A child who is yet to speak and unable to communicate, is at a steady state of rest and peace except for the normal uncomfortable moments which he is only able to communicate through cries.

The restless moments come when a child begins to gradually notice his environment and from a natural place of curiosity, begins to connect with the things around him using his five senses. This restlessness comes with growth and this growth is depicted in how much the child begins to respond to the environment and how much of this information the brain processes.

As children grow up, they gradually learn to express themselves and start to talk. Within a few years, they become inquisitive pre-schoolers with never ending questions. Questions build up in children tandem with development, and if you have been with a toddler, you will agree with me that they ask all sorts of questions. They want to know something about everything, which is not wrong; but they tend to improvise or seek answers elsewhere for the questions that don't get answered. The challenge here is with the quality of answers they find and if these are right or wrong answers.

With growth and development, adolescence, teenage years and adulthood set in, and this does not put an end to the questions, rather, it increases them. The difference is that instead of the questions being blurted out and directed to people randomly by a pre-schooler or primary schooler, teenagers will most likely keep their opinions to themselves or share only with those they have formed a strong bond and relationship with. And hopefully, they find confidants in good and godly people who give them right answers from God's perspective.

The implication of looking for answers in the wrong places and from the wrong people, is a downward spiral that could hold a person down for the most part of her life until she finds the right people with the right answers; and this is unfortunately not the case for most people. The accumulation of wrong answers and opinions form strongholds, incorrect mentalities and negative life-shaping characters.

This is not different for adults; everyone still has questions and some have mastered how to get the right answers from the right sources. These questions and what they are bordered around, however, is for an understanding of who we are as humans, an understanding of the world around us, and how we fit in.

This section on identity will provide a major shift in thoughts, insights and an understanding of your identity in its true sense.

The questions referred to above, which also burn in your heart, can be captured and summarized as questions of identity, fulfilment and significance in life. They are all centred around purpose and spirituality.

I recently saw a documentary on one of the world's most famous and youngest tennis players who after winning four grand slams, lost one. While talking about this single loss, she brought up the big question of existence and identity. Having built a life around her career, there was no room for more. However, this experience created the room for her to explore the more to life.

These questions are brought up by deep thoughts that most people would rather not bother with till they experience challenging situations that offset life as they see it. Thank God for such situations as it only leads to a critical evaluation of life, providing a more balanced, more fulfilling and more purposeful life.

Some of these defining questions are:

1. **Who am I?** From where did I originate before birth and where am I headed to after life as we know it now? This question relates to your *origin*.

2. **What am I here for?** Or what am I existing for? This relates to the discovery of your *purpose*.

3. **What can I do?** Or what will I be known for? This relates to living a life of *impact*.

4. **Where am I going?** Or where am I headed to? This has to do with your *destiny* and *destination*.

These questions elaborate on what purpose and a purposeful lifestyle means to us as individuals. We will look at these questions and answer them in detail in the coming sections.

That said, these are questions that can limit a person if such person does not get the right answers. These questions are silently brooding in everyone's heart and only seek answers from those who have gained self-mastery enough to want to live a more meaningful life; not a shallow, repetitive one that is void of true satisfaction at every stage. There is a satisfaction that should come with every stage of life as we go forward in life.

You would notice that the question around identity came first as should be, and it started with origin.

From our little child analogy and real-life scenarios, you would notice that before children begin a series of questions, they start somewhere around

There is a satisfaction that should come with every stage of life as we go forward in life.

identifying an object or subject of interest. That is, they first become curious and most likely name it or ask an adult for its name - an action that aids identification and again, brings us to identity. So, you are likely to get a lot of "what is that" or "who is that" questions from children at the developing ages of about 2 to 9 years. A trait that isn't farfetched in adults as well, as I already mentioned.

Purpose Action

Write down your answers to the four (4) defining questions above.

When you finish reading this book, do well to revisit and review the answers and adjust them where necessary to reflect what you have understood from reading this book.

CHAPTER TWO

DISCOVERING YOUR IDENTITY

"We need to be able to detach ourselves from the reality of
where we came through *into the earth in order to embrace
our identity as a function of* **where we came from**, *and
that origin is found in GOD."*

Now that we have had an overview of identity, we can answer the big WHAT and WHO questions. Ideally, we would begin our Identity Discovery journey with self-definition. We can do this by starting from the book of the beginnings (Genesis). Let's reflect on the story of the first man God created - Adam.

Our creation was in the same way as that of the first creation, with some slight changes that occurred after the first man fell (sinned) and got displaced. As a result of this, it was necessary that Jesus came as the perfect image of creation. He came to bridge the gap, first as God's perfect example to us and second, as the one from whom we should take the description of our identity.

When God created the first man, the very first expression He had concerning Adam and by extension, every other human, was the word **good.** The word good refers to something *to be desired or approved of.* Good could also describe a thing that *has the right requirements or which meets standard.* In production and manufacturing, meeting required standards is a big deal and the main essence of a product. Many times, this is termed as *the ability of a unit to be fit for purpose.* There are bodies who stand as authorities to enforce these predefined standards.

Next time you attempt to figure out who you are, you can easily think back on these descriptions. God knew the standards He had set for humans and He saw that achieved in who He made us originally. We came out good; immersed in all the depth, richness and meaning of the word 'good'; and God's plan is that we turn out good as we are shaped and refined whilst passing through life.

That one word – good, answers the vital identity question and this includes physical looks.

If your Creator describes you as good, you should find it hard to accept what anyone, especially a

God knew the standards He had set for humans and He saw that achieved in who He made us originally.

similarly created being as you, says about you, if it does not align with God's description of you. You are fit for purpose! You need to be grounded in this understanding and believe it wholly.

Before God declared that you are good, He already placed abilities, gifts, talents, and strengths in every man; the way He did for the first man, Adam. He gave Adam the responsibility and authority to dominate over the earth and everything in it. This answers another vital question that strengthens our grasp of identity as an attribute of the Creator in whose image we are made - **ability and capability**. This serves as a constant reminder that we can do absolutely anything we set our hearts and minds to, as the authority we have is dominion over all the earth!

YOU CAN. While you would not have to do everything that occurs to you or feels good to you, you can do all things. You might be wondering about the number of things you may have failed at, but be assured that no matter the circumstance or level of training, with the right amount of resilience, you can get anything and everything right.

> *"I can do all things [which He has called me to do] through Him who strengthens and empowers me [to fulfil His purpose—I am self-sufficient in Christ's sufficiency; I am ready for anything and equal to anything through Him who infuses me with inner strength and confident peace.]"*

Philippians 4:13, AMP

Ability - the capacity to be and to do is inbuilt. This understanding guided Adam to do as he was led to do, which was all he needed, and which also brought about abundance and satisfaction. Let me add here that only God could have pointed him to what to do; he did not use any inspiration or direction outside of God's. God did not only give him

> *We can do absolutely anything we set our hearts and minds to, as the authority we have is dominion over all the earth!*

his job description, but also made all he needed to be productive, effective, and prosperous available to him, including the woman who became his companion and helpmeet. Adam's life is what we can easily refer to as perfect, until he disobeyed the instructions he was given to live by.

Like in the stages we talked about from childhood to adulthood, he began to take note of his environment with questions in his heart. Eden, with man in it, was at a state of perfection so there were no questions in the beginning until the devil introduced questions to Eve and then Eve shared these questions with Adam. This can be found in the Bible in Genesis 3.

> *"1Now the serpent was more subtle than any beast of the field which the LORD God had made. And he said unto the woman, Yea, hath God said, Ye shall not eat of every tree of the garden? 2And the woman said unto the serpent, we may eat of the fruit of the trees of the garden: 3but of the fruit of the tree which is in the midst of the garden, God hath said, Ye shall not eat of it, neither shall ye touch it,*

lest ye die. 4*And the serpent said unto the woman, Ye shall not surely die:* 5*for God doth know that in the day ye eat thereof, then your eyes shall be opened, and ye shall be as gods, knowing good and evil.* 6*And when the woman saw that the tree was good for food, and that it was pleasant to the eyes, and a tree to be desired to make one wise, she took of the fruit thereof, and did eat, and gave also unto her husband with her; and he did eat."*

Genesis 1:1-6, KJV

The passage above speaks to how we should be careful, not only about the questions in our head as some might be misleading, but also be mindful of the source of these questions. Are the questions in your heart from God, from you or from the devil? Probe deeper until you find the root of the questions, thoughts and ideas in your heart. If you are a Thought Leader or you hold a position of influence over others, please do well to encourage people who look to you for answers to do the same.

Lack of identity takes away the access that should rightly belong to humans. For Adam, he had been exclusively under the care and cover of God in the beginning but ended up not knowing whose he was or who he was anymore. Studying the book of Genesis, you will realize more about his life and how it went from perfection - with him having all, to having nothing and starting all over, the beginning of a hustling to make ends meet - a different lifestyle from God's original purpose for mankind. Thankfully, there was a reversal that happened through the solution God brought to the world in the person of Christ Jesus. we are blessed to be part of a special dispensation that can now get things right. A dispensation that gets to experience God's privileges as the Creator and owner of all, over again. A dispensation that understands their identity with an experiential knowledge.

Let us look at the case study of Jesus: His beliefs and affirmations about His identity, as well as people's reactions to these.

Following the New Testament closely, there are different places where Jesus openly spoke about His identity. One of the things that endears me most to the lifestyle of Jesus is the fact that He always affirmed His identity - where He was from and how He had to follow the way and examples of His Heavenly Father.

The fact that He was the Son of God did not particularly make Him the people's favourite or their hero; He was neither more liked nor more respected by the masses. One thing, however, was glaring - He was never ignored. The knowledge of His identity made Him significant. To be specific, Jesus actually experienced more negativity from people whenever He affirmed His identity by proclaiming who He was out loud, but this never stopped Him! Eventually, several people started to see Him the way He saw Himself.

Here are some of Jesus's testimonies about Himself and people's reaction to it which we can still see today in how the world rejects the Truth.

> "Your father Abraham rejoiced to see My day, and he saw it and was glad." So, the Jews said to Him, "You are not yet fifty years old, and have You seen Abraham?" Jesus said to them, "Truly, truly, I say to you, before Abraham was born, I am."   John 8:56-58 ESV

"I and the Father are one." The Jews picked up stones again to stone Him. Jesus answered them, "I showed you many good works from the Father; for which of them are you stoning Me?" The Jews answered Him, "For a good work we do not stone You, but for blasphemy; and because You, being a man, make Yourself out to be God." John 10:30-39 NASB 1995

"There was a lot of grumbling about him among the crowds. Some argued, "He's a good man," but others said, "He's nothing but a fraud who deceives the people." But no one had the courage to speak favourably about him in public, for they were afraid of getting in trouble with the Jewish leaders. So, Jesus told them, "My message is not my own; it comes from God who sent me."

John 7:12-13,16. NLT

A second thing I noticed about Jesus's affirmation of His identity is that as He proclaimed it, despite the opposition, the people started to refer to Him as He referred to Himself and here are some examples of this as well.

> *"And immediately He began preaching about Jesus in the synagogues, saying, "He is indeed the Son of God!"* Acts 9:20 NLT

> *"Then Nathanael exclaimed, "Rabbi, you are the Son of God—the King of Israel!"*
>
> John 1:49 NLT

> *"Simon Peter answered, "You are the Messiah, the Son of the living God."* Matthew 16:16 NLT

These brought me to the realisation that what we speak out loud constantly, not only benefits others, but also strengthens our own convictions. You should not be bothered about who understands or does not understand or even criticizes you when you make bold, Biblical declarations about yourself with the knowledge of your identity. This is about you and your future, not anyone else. Knowing and affirming your identity does more for you than only having a head knowledge of it. Talking about it and acting like it, helps you believe it more; and for your heart and soul to come into congruence with what your head already knows. Dr Caroline Leaf, author of *The Perfect You*, attested to this.

What we speak out loud constantly, not only benefits others, but also strengthens our own convictions.

According to studies, the words we speak out loud configures our brains into believing them and not only that, it also helps us to function in these beliefs. There is a plant experiment about words and growth where in the same atmospheric and surrounding conditions, the same seeds were planted and taken care of in the same manner with the same amount of water and sunshine. However, one was spoken to positively and the other was not spoken to at all. In another case, one was spoken to negatively. The end result of the three seeds were distinctively different from one another as the one which was constantly spoken to positively did far better than the other two.

Imagine how much better you would be living – the improved version of what you should naturally be – when you accurately and consistently confess and affirm your identity.

Knowing and walking in your divinely ordained purpose and capabilities, with an accurate understanding of your identity, is the first concept and the core of the purpose pathfinder.

> *Knowing and walking in your divinely ordained purpose and capabilities, with an accurate understanding of your identity, is the first concept and the core of the purpose pathfinder.*

Without a firm grasp of identity, a man can still manage to attain greatness in life, but he will never be able to catch up with becoming the specific person he was designed to be, and the purpose for which he was created.

<u>Purpose Action</u>

1. Write down five (5) points on what you have discovered about your identity from the examples in this chapter.

2. How can you relate this discovery to your personal life and how can you practise what you now know?

UNDERSTANDING YOUR IDENTITY

"Understanding who you are by God is the most important foundational knowledge you will need in life and it comes by revelation."

A lot of ties and attachments can entangle a person who is fixated on the realities, facts and beliefs of her cultural and natural background, especially one who allows his or her identity to be shaped by such realties. There must be a conscious evolving from such mindsets in order to understand, enter into and walk in your divinely ordained identity.

Spiritual Adoption

There was a break in the link that connected us directly to God when the first man sinned, and there was a gift from God that mended this broken link and brought us back in line with Him. The process of being joined back to God via Jesus, the Way, is what I refer to as Spiritual Adoption in this section.

We started this section on identity with the story of Adam and how he fell in sin by disobedience. However, God still cares deeply and has a covenant of wholeness and wellness for everyone who finds his or her way back to Him. The only way you can be detached from the default identity traced to the first man is by Spiritual Adoption.

There had to be another first man who had to be born of a woman but without the seed of a man. He is named Jesus and His coming, as ordained by God, changes the course of life of everyone who believes in Him and invests in understanding his identity through Him and in Him.

Before then, The Creator in His divine plans reached out to mankind again through Abraham. The Bible shows us the covenant God cut with Abraham, and you should take time to study about this by reading the book of Genesis chapter 15. This was after Abraham had carefully followed the leading and directions of God. From when God called Abraham in Genesis 12, you would notice that despite all the difficulties he endured, he kept his faith and focus and later became the bearer of the new covenant. We are all recipients of this covenant today.

If you are wondering how you are or could be connected to this covenant, the answer is through the Spiritual Adoption that happens when we accept the Lordship of Jesus and believe in Him and His assignment here on Earth. Jesus - who is God in human form, is God's perfect solution. Let us look into this in detail.

Your Spiritual Adoption is where your identity originated from. In a hierarchical diagram it would look like this:

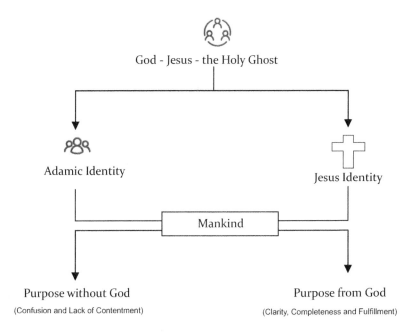

God - Jesus - the Holy Ghost

Adamic Identity

Jesus Identity

Mankind

Purpose without God
(Confusion and Lack of Contentment)

Purpose from God
(Clarity, Completeness and Fulfillment)

From the chart above, you will see that the choice of who we are, which ultimately determines where we draw purpose from, depends on whose identity we choose to conform to – Jesus's or Adam's.

Among others, two points we can deduce from the chart above are:

1. Adam came from God as part of creation and everyone else was procreated after him but he broke his link with God along the line (due to disobedience) and this led to consequences for all mankind.

2. Jesus came to the world as both God and man, with a direct link to God. He also came in a different way, not the Adamic procreation process. He came as part of the God-head.

This is why conforming your identity to the Adamic mandate is on the opposite side of conforming to your God-identity through Jesus. The result of who you identify with is that finding your purpose in life will either be from the Creator – in God, or outside of God, grasping for glimpses of fulfilment from the world as led by the god of this world. This is the ultimate result of relying on your Adamic capabilities only, outside of God's blueprint.

Purpose outside of God might seem like it but if it is not fulfilling the Creator's desires, it is not it.

The choice of your identity is dependent on you. You either receive the adoption of God through Christ to become God's own, or you deny this which by default links you to the sinful Adamic nature with a broken link to God. There is no guarantee of living in your authentic identity or a complete and purposeful life outside of God. Jesus is the only direct link to God for He was already with God from the beginning as the Triune God.

The choice of whom to model one's life after is a choice everyone would make unconsciously, subconsciously, or consciously; and each choice, at the end of life, takes mankind back to God in reward or judgement. You already know the significance of these choices, so, which do you choose?

The result of choosing the Adamic nature over Christ's nature, is confusion and lack of contentment. No matter how great what you attain in life is, there will be a void in your heart, like the hole in the middle of a doughnut. A life devoid of Christ is incomplete. The confusion will be like a mist of darkness; you may not even realise that it's

> *The result of choosing the Adamic nature over Christ's nature, is confusion and lack of contentment. No matter how great what you attain in life is, there will be a void in your heart, like the hole in the middle of a doughnut. A life devoid of Christ is incomplete.*

there, but you'd know something isn't right. On the other hand, choosing the life, identity and inheritance of Jesus, brings you into the light (revelation knowledge, understanding) and satisfaction that comes with being a child of God and this will launch you into living a purpose-driven life as God originally designed for you. You come in sync with God and this is the assurance of living in purpose daily.

The scriptures talk about how God adopted us into becoming His sons in the book of Ephesians 1:4-8 AMPC. *"Even as [in His love] He chose us [actually picked us out for Himself as His own] **in Christ** (Jesus) before the foundation of the world, that we should be holy (consecrated and set apart for Him) and blameless in His sight, even above reproach, before Him in love."*

Now, this only applies to those who have accepted Jesus Christ as their Lord and personal saviour, for it is only through Jesus Christ that this is effective.

The covenant God has with His chosen people goes as far back as when He made the promise to Abraham in Genesis 17:1-8, and He constantly emphasised this through the Israelites' journeys. These stories are well summarised in the Psalm of King David in the Bible (Psalm 78:105). After many generations, God kept reaffirming this covenant and promises and it has remained consistent. There is a covering that cannot compare to any other protection within any other capacity that is upon the offspring of Abraham and the Nation which God promised to build through him, which is the Israel of today.

You come into the equation of this covenant when you choose the fully victorious life of Christ which joins you to God's lineage as His son or daughter. This happens by a conscious choice to accept the life Jesus offered and affirming Him as your Lord, thereby cutting off from the Adamic line into Christ's line (Romans 10:9,10). This makes you become an heir of the promises God gave to the Israelites and our claim to it through Christ Jesus.

"Jesus saith unto him, I am the way, the truth, and the life: no man cometh unto the Father, but by me". John 14:6. KJV (Ephesians 2, Hebrews 6, Colossians 2).

Being connected to God through Jesus is what sets the tone for a truly purposeful life. The decision to choose Jesus and grow in Him by feeding on God's word in the Bible, rather than continue with the Adamic line, begins a heart work within you. This work is synonymous to the physical circumcision that was done on the Israelites as the Jewish tradition. This heart work is the spiritual circumcision that configures you to live the new life befitting of the sons of God, and that is your identity.

The negative consequence of Adam's disobedience and the curse is what Jesus comes into your life to take away with your agreement and cooperation. This is what gives us access again into the fullness of God and the purpose life. **This is a major purpose pathfinder as a person may be very successful and yet live very empty and tormenting personal and inter-personal lives.** Purpose in Christ makes life wholesome and balanced with the proper knowledge. This knowledge is the package you are getting in this book.

While the fallen nature through Adam will incorporate the creativity for economic impact making, ground-breaking innovation, market expertise and career progression, the new life in Christ Jesus brings the balance of the life of God and inspiration from the mind of God through the Holy Spirit into the equation. Purpose will be knowing the true worth and enjoying the applicable benefits from what you have and are doing in your spirit, soul and body.

We inherited both the blessing and the curse from the Adamic nature but the new life in Christ brings a curse-cancellation blessing into our lives that make us to now operate again at the level of God as we were initially designed to do.

Living in the Adamic without the new life is what brings about the flows of satanic and demonic inspirations to the world. It brings the kind of results that stem from the works

> *We inherited both the blessing and the curse from the Adamic nature but the new life in Christ brings a curse-cancellation blessing into our lives that make us to now operate again at the level of God as we were initially designed to do.*

of darkness and spiritual wickedness which binds up seemingly well-to-do individuals in shackles of mind trickery and deceptions that lead to more works of wickedness, decadence and death.

The entire 10th Chapter of the book of John in the Bible clarifies what Jesus has done to free us from this as the devil works freely with the soul land of unsaved men who are merely guided by the good inherited from Adam. The coming of Jesus and our acceptance of Jesus' love and forgiveness, introduces God into our good; the intentional cultivation of this life of God in our souls uproots every work the devil has planted there as a consequence of the sinful nature.

Look Inward

> *"Your vision will become clear only when you can look into your own heart. Who looks outside dreams, who looks inside awakens."*

> —Carl Jung

Looking inward through the lens of God's eternal counsel for you, is how you solidify the knowledge of your origin in God and adoption into Him. And yes, with choosing the birthright of Jesus, you are linked to God who created you and can begin to see yourself the way He sees you. What the understanding of your identity can do for your purpose, will only be discovered as you look inwards and lean into God.

God has become your origin if you've accepted the life of Christ. It is common for us to look around ourselves and make comparisons or desire to be like others whom we admire. While this is not wrong as an action, it comes from a wrong logic which often leads to the wrong conclusions. It is second nature for most humans to want to compare themselves with others and this is why the Bible also warns about it. Who you are, who you should be and what you should be seeing concerning your life, can only be revealed to you when you look inward.

Looking outside will make you aspire to be who you were not meant to be because everyone's journey is unique. I grew up seeing a lot of competition among adults and children alike. However, since children by nature pick things up so quickly, we can say that competition originated from what they see the adults around them do.

You see someone starting a new business and you automatically 'discover' that business was meant for you, or you find someone employing a strategy and you believe you are to use the same strategy – this only makes you an imitator at best. When you have a mentality of God's abundance, you can be confident about your personal ideas and seeking God's face for leadings, directions and answers original to you. These might end up looking similar to someone else's, but you'd know for certain where and how you sourced for it. In the same manner, you will not be bothered about being imitated because you know more will come from where the current one came from and likewise, you won't depend on imitating others because you know that your inheritance in Christ Jesus has all the spiritual, physical and creative provisions and power you can ever need, and much more.

Who you are, who you should be and what you should be seeing concerning your life, can only be revealed to you when you look inward.

For the person who has made a lifestyle of imitating or copying others, who told you that you can't get an idea that is original to you? Replace that knowledge with the right one. God is abundant towards you.

God is still in the business of giving dreams, ideas and witty inventions if we decide to look inward and not outward. As a matter of fact, He created us with these in mind. I call it our **God deposits**.

Your vision for your life is unique to you, it does not have to come from what you see others do. Looking inward would mean you looking into and understanding your identity – your total make up - as this knowledge will help you to understand how different you are from others. You will also understand how to channel your difference/uniqueness into receiving your own specific mode of operation in your field of expertise. It doesn't matter how similar what you do is to that of another person, no two persons are ever the same; your unique DNA adds a different flavour to what you have sourced out correctly even if it looks like someone else's.

Looking inward will not only give you your own divine strategy, it will equally provide all you need to carry it out, including your own tribe of loyal people who will help you accomplish all you desire without any *hassles*. It is a special kind of ease and bliss.

Looking inward is a proven method of drawing out grace. Also, He who is within you (talking about God within you) is greater than he who you are looking at outwardly (1 John 4:4). It is a credit to your personality to think for yourself. You owe it to yourself to dig out from the depths of intelligence within you. Don't wait around for other people to do it for themselves and then you copy it. You can invest in personal development and coaching opportunities to discover more about yourself.

Purpose Action

1. Set apart segments of your day, twice a day, to intentionally lock out every irrelevancy to what you have to do at the moment, then reflect and focus on God fully – looking inward to receive His direction for your life.

2. As you do this, you would find divinely inspired ideas on immediate next steps dropping in your heart.

Pray with this and run with it as it gets impressed more strongly in your heart over the days.

What You See Is What You Get

This is not a sentence that only works for programming, it also works for our lifestyles. Somewhere along the line in search of our identity, we all held on to different views which gave us different perspectives to life, either from a negative or positive angle. Ultimately, your perspective and beliefs become your experience.

Since dreams come true, why not dream bigger? Choose to live with a blind spot to whatever holds you down; look beyond this and dream bigger! Some hold on to their doctor's or physician's report, some hold on to their teacher's or counsellor's reports, and some others hold on to the thoughts the devil has long whispered into their ears and minds. Remember, you don't just get what you see, but also what you believe.

Perhaps, you don't know how the beliefs you hold on to got there but you've been holding on to the lies. You even go as far as defending some of these beliefs without a thought because you respect the person whose opinion of you it was. Have you looked inwards or even better, asked your Creator how true those opinions are?

Many people have allowed themselves to be defined by the negative tags and words they have been called, like *stupid, good for nothing, timid, Blacksheep, addict;* or to be named after a health or physical condition. While some of these are temporary conditions, most of these, sadly, came from people whom they might hold or have held dearly in the past. It is our responsibility to consciously come out of these labels. And this is possible by the power of the sacrifices Jesus made, IF you choose to believe in them. All you have to do is hold tightly to and constantly re-affirm your true identity from God's perspective. This perspective is well stated in several portions of the Bible; if you need a place to start from, you can begin here - *"I thank you because I am awesomely made, wonderfully; your works are wonders– I know tis very well."* Psalm 139:14 CJB

While some of the opinions mentioned earlier might be indisputable facts from medical perspectives or noticeable physical or otherwise traits, there is no truth in them. Facts greatly differ from truths and you need to be guided by this. For instance, if your doctors confirm for a fact that you have a condition and because of that you won't be able to do certain things in life, or you are believed to be at some disadvantage due to a physical attribute; those are mere facts that are not tied to you or qualify as a definition of you. You have to let go of this baggage to discover the truth of who you truly are which can be found in God alone. You are not tied to those opinions and you should definitely let go of them in order to allow the real you come alive from your spirit within you.

> *"For what person knows the thoughts and motives of a man except the man's spirit within him? So also no one knows the thoughts of God except the Spirit of God. Now we have received, not the spirit of the world, but the [Holy] Spirit who is from God, so that we may know and understand the [**wonderful**] things freely given to us by God."*

1 Corinthians 2:11-12 AMP

What the truth is and would always be, is what God has said about you. This can be uncovered by God's spirit at work in you as you study God's word. One thing I love in the scripture above is the word 'wonderful'; it gives the assurance that God has not only prepared things for us but wonderful things as our Father and one who loves us dearly! Feel free to imagine and reflect on these wonderful acts from God! He has also said in another portion of the scriptures that you are called out of darkness into His marvellous light: *"But you are a chosen generation, a royal priesthood, a holy nation, His own special people, that you may proclaim the praises of Him who called you out of darkness into His marvellous light;* 1 Peter 2:9 NKJV. *"[The Father] has delivered and drawn us to Himself out of the control and the dominion of darkness and has transferred us into the kingdom of the Son of His love."* Colossians 1:13 AMPC

This next scripture talks about the good works (works to be desired of or approved of, that have the right requirements or meets standard) we were created for:

> *"For we are his workmanship, created in Christ Jesus unto good works, which God hath before ordained that we should walk in them."* Ephesians 2:10 KJV

I think this is an amazing package we came in, the authentic packaging that unravels us. There are many scriptures in the Bible that talk about the esteem God holds you in and the many blessings He has declared concerning your life. However, it is your duty to seek them out, believe them and walk in their reality. What you must do now is hold tightly to the word of God and you will see it happen in your life.

Many things have been said about many people which turned out to be false as they rose above those situations; they chose to believe only what God had said about them. Kenneth Hagin is an example of a man like you and I who rose above his doctor's predictions on his deathbed to live several decades more and do several great works that touches generations even generations unborn. He started believing God and God's power as his Creator over his doctors' power and predictions. You have absolutely no obligation to be held down by other people's definition of you.

Again, all you need do is search God's word – the Bible, and receive the Words He has spoken about you and over you. Believe The Word, confess it and act on it. It is that simple. When you frame your identity around your Creator's intention for you, you will see it play out excellently in your life.

An understanding of our identity, ordination, baptism, and calling, is an invitation to walk in the full expression of who we are by Creation. I want you to know that without understanding your identity, you are likely to live a very strenuous life regardless of your looks, intellect or inherited wealth. This is as a function of the internal aspect that has direct evidence on your outward life and different manifestations or expressions. Without a clear sense and an in-depth understanding of the unique you, a realization of who created you and for what purpose, the devil is ready to constantly have a field day on your mind, and any little negative experience you have could affect you more than you know. This is why some have died by suicide or wrong influences because they didn't have a clear sense of their identity. The words and actions of external influences had too much internal impact on them.

> *When you frame your identity around your Creator's intention for you, you will see it play out excellently in your life.*

Their physical conditions and circumstances pushed them too far when they could have been propelled forward and above by the words and promises of God. Why not say a few words of prayer for clarity of your purpose and identity now, thanking God for whom He has called you and what He has said about you.

Purpose Action

Craft your identity from the scriptures by taking out a portion of your day to prayerfully research the scriptures daily for the next 21 days. As you do so, receive the Word God highlights to you and like Jeremiah did, describe yourself with this identity - the way God declares it. Let this word strengthen your spirit daily.

> *"'For I know the plans and thoughts that I have for you,' says the Lord, 'plans for peace and well-being and not for disaster, to give you a future and a hope.'"*

Jeremiah 29:11 AMP.

Your Identity Can Be Exclusive Of Your Circumstances

We have established what your identity means and what it doesn't, but in wrapping things up, let's talk about how you still feel because you need to clarify these feelings.

Irrespective of your circumstances, current or past, one thing you must always be aware of is that who you are is independent of what has happened to you.

Adam's identity included his nationality so we could say, Eden – the first place of habitation that God prepared for man. He had a close tie with God as His Father, Master and Creator. However, the result of Adam's ban from the presence of God and the place God had prepared and put him in, must have made him lose the literal sense, feel and meaning of his identity. Leaving Eden for the wilderness along with his family, and with no hope of going back there, would have been a confusing situation for him. Let me add here that a wilderness season is never the problem as it could be the perfect place to reach out to the Creator and get on track.

Another example here is the case of Jesus. This is because His reality didn't entirely look like His

> *Irrespective of your circumstances, current or past, one thing you must always be aware of is that who you are is independent of what has happened to you.*

identity which made many question His being the Son of God. The Jews at the time expected the Son of God to look different or act differently but that would defeat Jesus's coming as a man and also as God's incarnate. This was too much for the Jews to believe but that did not alter Jesus being the Son of God, or His knowledge of who He is and the demonstration of His power with simplicity.

This is not to say you should look different from who you really are; however, there should be harmony and congruence within you that affirms your authenticity. This would naturally flow out of you in the physical once you are spiritually connected to your true identity. In the case of Jesus, it was the people whom He came to save who had a different view and perception of Him due to the expectations they had built in their minds and their cultural beliefs. This is however an attestation to prophecy which had to be fulfilled.

As you begin to understand and accept your true identity in Christ, you will begin to see this reflect all over you.

You might be wondering how to own up to your identity. It begins simply by *saying it, believing it and acting it.* I started with saying because people sometimes find it hard to believe what they have not seen. It is easier when you keep saying it to yourself. Eventually, you would hear it from your own mouth so many times that you now believe it and begin to act like it until you see it. This is also when other people begin to see it as well but don't be disturbed about what people see at the beginning of your manifestation. You are still emerging.

How people perceive you is not as important as how you perceive yourself. The knowledge of your identity and how you perceive yourself, can totally make or mar your journey into living a purposeful life by God's standards.

More often than not, things aren't the same as they seem - we tend to over analyse or exaggerate things, or have false perceptions. So, next time you believe a thing that is not aligned with your identity, ask yourself who told you so? The only thing that should be magnified in your eyes and emphasised by your mouth is the ever living, ever true Word and promises of God concerning you.

> *The only thing that should be magnified in your eyes and emphasised by your mouth is the ever living, ever true Word and promises of God concerning you.*

There was a great man in the scriptures who was not perceived in line with his identity. In fact, he was described in a completely different way from the impact of his life and the way he lived to the fullness of his potential and purpose. His name is Paul.

Paul was not unaware of the way that others saw him and spoke about him; but he wouldn't say that about himself, neither would he compare or class himself with others. Paul had a very clear sense of his identity and purpose and was aware and intentional about living purposefully. He knew there was no wisdom in competition. *"I may seem to be boasting too much about the authority given to us by the Lord. But our authority builds you up; it doesn't tear you down. So, I will not be ashamed of using my authority. I'm not trying to frighten you by my letters. For some say, "Paul's letters are demanding and forceful, but in person he is weak, and his speeches are worthless!" Those people should realize that our actions when we arrive in person will be as forceful as what we say in our letters from far away. Oh, don't worry; we wouldn't dare say that we are as wonderful as these other men who tell you how important they are! But they are only comparing themselves with each other, using themselves as the standard of measurement. How ignorant!" 2 Corinthians 10:12, MSG*

Let nothing, absolutely nothing, hinder you - be it others perception of you or your perception of yourself. Be fully all that God has made you to be, be determined to fulfil your purpose in grand style.

In getting your identity right, it is important to know your source. If you still believe you came from an ape or from science without any form of supernatural connection, then you are still getting it wrong. This would mean there is nothing more to you than what can be seen on the exterior and all that is attributed to your anatomy. There is a spirit in your body which cannot be seen. There is also a soul within you which receives the content of your spirit, alongside what you allow to form your physical experiences; it uses this information to shape your thought patterns and responses. None of the above could be a result of an animal changing form into another or anything else Science might want to explain it to be. It is a deliberate and divine crafting by the only Supreme Being.

Remember, you cannot have the correct understanding of your identity without recognizing your source – where you pre-existed from. We all came into the world with our uniqueness, we are not superior to one another, we are only different from one another. It is therefore our sole responsibility to discover who we are and how we differ from one another, respecting and embracing it.

Asides the distinguishing differences we all have, like our unique fingerprints and DNA, every man must explore and experience his own awesomeness.

Purpose Action

1. With your understanding of identity from what you have learnt so far, list out the words you have previously identified yourself with which are not in line with God's description of you.

2. Now replace each of these descriptions with the truth of the current understanding you now have. Go through the difference between the old and the new often in order to have a clear mental image of the transformation happening in you.

You now know who you are according to your Creator's specifications in the Bible. Begin to constantly say it, believe it and act like it.

In conclusion, while we have our similarities, we absolutely don't have to keep defining ourselves from other people's perspectives or perception. Think about this: with who or from where do you still identify yourself in relation to sameness? Your parents, your tribe or your Creator? See Revelation 5:9.

> *"And they sung a new song, saying, Thou art worthy to take the book, and to open the seals thereof: for thou wast slain,* **and hast redeemed us to God by thy blood out of every kindred, and tongue, and people, and nation;"** Revelation 5:9. KJV

This was a conclusion from the finished works of Christ to re-connect us to our source and establish our new identity from His sacrifice. That new identity that redefines us after the fall and sinful nature resulted in a new name, a new kinship, a new tongue/language, and a new Nationality. Revelation 5:9 is what should naturally define us in our new identity. The last paragraph specifically mentions redemption and this is the end product of the entire process Jesus went through on earth. He did it all to redeem us from whatever previous state or position our tribe, tongue, nation and people had kept us in, in the past. He gave us a new identity! This identity is what that scripture has given to me and that is how I have incorporated it into my life and family.

Identity As A Proof Of Identification

The final definition we'd look at in this concluding chapter on Identity is, identity as a proof of identification. This can be likened to what an ID card will contain and I believe 9 out of every 10 adults will have at least one form of identification card. You can check out what is on your ID card right now if you have it handy. You would find that it contains the basic information about you as a person: who you are, your parents or spouse's name, where you're from, your origin or nationality, age, ethnicity and so on.

Naturally, your identity is a combination of your DNA and other factors but supernaturally, your identity is who you are as God's own son or daughter.

As a supernatural being, your identity has now become a function of who God calls you and is no longer subject to what others, including you, have called yourself.

Let us look at another Bible personality who experienced a change in identity: Jacob. Although he was named Jacob by his parents, after the encounter he had with God, his name was changed from Jacob to Israel. He was still called Jacob but everything about him now responded to and reflected the name Israel. The intention and motive behind this name were a Nation which became his reality in the end. He aligned to his new identity and literally became the foundation of the Nation of Israel. You should be aware that this happened after the encounter with His Creator - this is why you cannot operate in and begin to replicate your identity until you have taken out some time to connect with God. We cannot talk about subjects like the identity and purpose of man without considering the Master and Creator of it.

There is an evident peace you experience when you get things right in life. It is a deep-seated peace that embodies and shields you from being overwhelmed by the issues of life. This peace is a result of a deep-seated understanding of your identity. You will be led by this peace that comes from knowing you are God's own and you would come to experience the tangible presence and leading of God as a Father when you know you are of Him and from Him. This has been my experience, a steadiness deep in my heart, that has come from being led into God's purpose for my life daily and progressively.

It is a journey, and you will receive more insights by the help of the Holy Spirit as you sit with this. One of my greatest desires in life is to live according to God's purpose for my life and He has given me the mandate of sharing how to do this with you so let us find out more in the next section of this book – PART 2: STEPPING INTO PURPOSE.

> *We cannot talk about subjects like the identity and purpose of man without considering the Master and Creator of it.*

<u>Purpose Action</u>

1. Assess your physical identity in relation to what you have discovered from the previous Purpose Actions and find out what you already manifest and what you do not yet manifest.

PART TWO

STEPPING INTO PURPOSE

CHAPTER FOUR

GOD DEPOSITS

"Creations don't just happen, they are designed."

In every intricate design, every part has a purpose, a story and a process. Nothing is just as it seems – everything is the way it is for a reason. Knowing this is knowing peace, it is knowing what you were wired for and the reason you were wired the way you are. Now that you know who you are, you should know what God has deposited in you and what it is meant for.

Many people are neck-deep into doing good works but the good works are not the right work they should be committing their lives to. It is like the case of zeal without knowledge but in this case, without purpose.

There is already enough confusion around what a person should be doing with his or her life. The pressure begins when children are asked what they want to become in the future. While it is not wrong to spark a child's curiosity and let him begin to lean into an area of expertise or an aspect of life, you should do a better job of it by helping the child to first know and become secure in who he is, what he is capable of and then guide him to discover his unique strengths. With the right empowerment, this is a discovery and an empowerment that can be attained by careful observation of all God has deposited in us.

We will still look into discovery of our unique giftings as part of God's deposits and these are life-long learnings which can begin as early as possible. The light starts to dawn and discovery begins as soon as we begin to pay cognisance to our deposits from God.

If you are currently ruminating on what precisely you should be committed to and what your good works are, you will find for yourself that doing a lot in life is not as important as doing what counts; and what counts is what we have been specifically designed for by God, using what He has deposited in us specifically for that purpose.

What matters most, what counts and what a person should invest her life into doing, is what God has intended for such one to do, which is her purpose. This is what we need to engage our energy in and dedicate our time to. It comes from our internal deposit account, where God keeps depositing and we keep withdrawing from. It is His mission; it accomplishes His will and it is backed by His power. It is not about our success but God's success!

Intricately Designed

We started this chapter with a quote that says, "Creations don't just happen". Let's interact with this vivid example from the scriptures which speaks to God's deposits in us as the originator/perpetuator of this creation called humans.

> "Now the Lord said to Moses, "See,
> I have called by name Bezalel, son
> of Uri, the son of Hur, of the tribe
> of Judah. I have filled him with the
> Spirit of God in wisdom and skill,
> in understanding and intelligence,

in knowledge, and in all kinds of craftsmanship, to make artistic designs for work in gold, in silver, and in bronze, and in the cutting of stones for settings, and in the carving of wood, to work in all kinds of craftsmanship. And behold, I Myself have appointed with him Oholiab, son of Ahisamach, of the tribe of Dan; to all who are wise-hearted I have given the skill and ability to make everything that I have commanded you:"

Exodus 31:1-6 AMP.

From the above, we clearly see and can deduce that God has intentionally designed every human with unique skills just like Bezalel from the scripture above. This is a vivid example of God's deposits. God went ahead to advise Moses who needed the skillset at the time that this was a man who was made for the job.

Bezalel in this scripture, might not even know the extent to which God had invested and deposited in him. We are minefields of all that is needed to excel at our individual areas of expertise, which need to be discovered, mined and refined for use.

> *We are minefields of all that is needed to excel at our individual areas of expertise, which need to be discovered, mined and refined for use.*

Consider your areas of specialization and expertise, if you already have one or more, and list out all the human requirements that are needed to be successful in that field. Guess what? You have everything in that list in you! Like Bezalel, you have wisdom and skill in understanding and intelligence, in knowledge, and in all kinds of craftsmanship. If you have all the skill, talent, wisdom and understanding from God like it was discovered in the Bible passage above, and then go on to pursue a different career or calling asides God's intention and outside your skills and talents, no sense of purpose can come from that; it will only be a pursuit out of alignment.

I would like to note that as I mention career in this book, I talk about it from an angle of living purposefully as God created man to live - with a mandate to work. So, your workplace excellence is symbolic to your career in these illustrations. Work is one of the main essences of life. Life only operates after God spoke it into existence because we operate it. The way we operate life is by work! Work is you and I operating the highly complex and diverse machinery of life, and purposeful work makes the operation of life beautiful and fit for individual use as we work it out.

> *"And God blessed them, saying, be fruitful, and multiply, and fill the waters in the seas, and let fowl multiply in the earth."*
>
> Genesis 1:22 KJV

I understand, however, that not everyone will live their best lives from the career angle, and many don't even follow the career pathway. So, be it career or any other work and mode your life takes, that does not alter what is being said here or make it inapplicable to you. Afterall, purpose is in itself living life according to God's mandate and blueprint for your life. In the same vein, career to some is not the white- or blue--collar vertical path to a peak others pursue, but just taking a day at a time and investing their best in their offspring or other such priceless vocations (calling, career aptitude).

Picking from the example of the likes of Jeremiah, Bezalel and other patriarchs from the Bible, I am convinced that God wouldn't bless some people so much and put nothing at all in some others. That does not just align with the nature of God as seen in the Bible and as experienced by us. Definitely not! What surfaces, however, is that many have failed to understand their purpose, discover their identity or recognize their giftings. We see in different places where patriarchs of old such as David and Jeremiah, spoke with so much clarity and understanding, how God was deliberate about them, knowing them before they started to actually exist, and already had plans for them.

> *I am convinced that God wouldn't bless some people so much and put nothing at all in some others.*

Jeremiah understood that God formed him in his mother's womb and therefore knew him before he knew himself. He went ahead to affirm that he knew the plans God had for him and that they are good ones. He was able to catch God's blueprint for his life in the preceding verse and understood his purpose and the assignment that would lead to that purpose in this blueprint.

> *"Jeremiah, I am your Creator, and before you were born, I chose you to speak for me to the nations."*
> Jeremiah 1:5, CEV
> *"I will bless you with a future filled with hope—a future of success, not of suffering."*
> Jeremiah 29:11 CEV.

What an assurance!

David stated that God knew the number of hairs on his head. This shows us the intentionality of God when it comes to His creation. More than this, the specificity of all that we would need to excel in an area of expertise has been incorporated into God's design of us. David was a spectacular king and Jeremiah was a powerful prophet. All that was premeditated by God was revealed and available to them with all they needed deposited in them before time. This is true for every single person and the revelation of this is possible.

It is important to note here that they discovered these things for themselves, and they affirmed it. Their affirmation of what they believed proved as the assurance of what they said.

Scenario 1:

I had a conversation with an old friend a long time ago where she was sharing with me, convinced that she had no talent. She went further to state that the wrong habits and misfortunes she had experienced were her talents I.e., what she did best, like losing things and so on. Today she is doing well in her career and she also has a clothing line! In retrospect, I can tell she transformed her thinking at some point in her life or she got help to fix the previous negative mindset.

I am certain that at some points in our lives, we have felt this way. It could be from a sense of insecurity or hints of envy from when you see other people doing certain things with some sort of ability you do not seem to have. It could be from a low self-esteem, and it could be for no apparent reason at all.

I remember being sympathetic with this friend and when I think about it now, I realize how ridiculous and laughable it was. I can tell you today, for sure, without any iota of doubt, that every single person has a unique skill from God that is deposited in her. While I will emphasize later in this book how your assignments aid in fulfilling your overall purpose, it is very possible that you are walking in purpose already by the works you are involved in without knowing it. There is no part of your story that is a waste. You might not be doing it well yet, but the parts of your journey are for specific purposes especially if you have allowed the leadership of God and the Lordship of Jesus; your process is precious to God.

As you pay attention, you will find out more and begin to see more vividly the deposits God has put inside you, including your unique abilities and assignments, and all the other details that lead to your purpose and help you live it out.

Your process is precious to God.

Purpose Action

1.   Affirm constantly and confidently that you have God's deposits inside you. Emphasize that it's in you and begin to see it manifest by watching out for it.

Scenario 2:

Let us go back to the example of Adam, God's first creation. God had placed in him the ability to do a great job at overseeing the garden and it is not surprising that this is the job God gave him. Adam was equipped for the assignment as it concerned him at the time. No wonder he did it excellently. He was where he should be and he discovered that he had the ability, therefore, he was able to apply this knowledge in carrying out his assignment. He did not just oversee the garden but tended to it.

Do you now agree with me that every man definitely has deposits from God in him even though this might be unknown to him? Some call it abilities; I see it as an unction to function. If there is any assignment before you right now, something you know can be done but not sure yet if you can do it or how to do it, tell yourself that: "I have the ability, unction and anointing to do this right and I will find out what it is that I need because I know who I am."

You most definitely have God's abilities within you.

Purpose Action

Make it your responsibility and set an assignment to reflect on your life - by observation and enquiry, to discover how much God loves you and what He has deposited in you to be your unique self.

CHAPTER FIVE

RECOGNIZING YOUR GOD DEPOSITS

Now that you know what God's deposits are all about, how do you recognize them? It is one thing to know a thing exists and it is another thing to find it out. One of the most amazing discoveries you will have in life is discovering what God placed in you that makes you unique. It is even better when you help others in the process of discovering theirs, or find help in others with discovering yours.

Now, we are aware that we all have God's deposits in us as a fact, how do we recognize

> *One of the most amazing discoveries you will have in life is discovering what God placed in you that makes you unique.*

them? This discovery is our individual jobs to do. However, we need the Creator to show us these blueprints alongside God's inspired professionals who will help us connect the dots.

The first step to insightful understanding of the deposits within us, and one thing I will keep emphasizing throughout this book, is to start by knowing our Creator because only He has our blueprint for life and living. We live in a society that is delusional. There are two extremes: those who believe we have all things put together and in perfect shape without any recognition for He who holds all things together – the Triune God. The other extreme believes nothing is working and no one is safe. Both extremes have a common belief of not acknowledging God the Master minder and planner of all.

God already put all that is needed to keep working out His plans for humanity and the earth in us and one way to recognize our God-deposits is by connecting with Him and creating a relationship with Him. *"For in Him was created the universe of things, both in the heavenly realm and on the earth, all that is seen and all that is unseen. Every seat of power, realm of government, principality, and authority—it all exists through Him and for His purpose!"* Colossians 1:16 TPT

There is an underlying mindset in most people that it is easier to connect with men whom we can see, than a God who we cannot see. But this is not true. If anything, the opposite is correct because we do not have to see God to have a relationship with Him. I talk specifically about this in my podcast, *The Anointed Series by Faith Ehira* – it's available on most podcast apps. I recommend that you find some time to check it out. If you want to learn more about building a relationship with your Creator and how to maintain it, these podcasts will come in handy. I mentioned earlier that you can discover your uniqueness by careful observation; you will also find out how to do that through the podcasts.

> *God already put all that is needed to keep working out His plans for humanity and the earth in us and one way to recognize our God-deposits is by connecting with Him and creating a relationship with Him.*

Purpose Action

Write out carefully and prayerfully, the repeated nudges you have in your heart to try out something new, both in familiar areas as well as in new areas. This is the starting point to making your abilities recognizable to you.

Dig Deeper!

As we conclude this chapter, let's review your experience with the last purpose action.

- Was it easy to know and follow the nudges in your heart? Why?

- Do you have any nudges in your heart to do new things or continue your existing positive acts?

These questions are to find out and address the root of and the importance of having a growing relationship with God. This is so key because the connection to discerning our gifts and callings excellently can only be deposited into our spirit when we have this connection. You don't want a pull or nudging that is not from God, Your Creator; neither do you want a complete lack of inspiration or new nudges to step up higher. I am talking about a Spirit-to-spirit connection here. One that does not begin from our external realities such as what we can hear, see or what is filtered into our minds from our senses.

One way you can identify your talents and skills are from the gifts, services and helps you have rendered with expertise to humanity. However, without a conscious awareness of this, you would be amazing and not even know what distinguishes you. To identify these graces and deposits within you, is self-mastery, and you need to continually dig deeper to keep getting it. By digging deeper, I mean asking yourself difficult questions, answering them and asking some more questions.

Digging deeper is the way you think intentionally: What did I just do there? Why do I speak this way? Why do I analyse things like this? Why do I look at people from this lens of kindness or curiosity or inquisitiveness? Why, What, How, Why and Why again.

Keep asking these questions and you are digging deeper, you are exploring your awesomeness and excavating the goodness within you to a surface level where it is visible to you and useful to everyone else.

There's Something For You Too, Even You!

There is an underlying mentality a lot of people low-key have but no one actually talks about. This mentality is the thought that greatness, excellence or a certain kind of high life, are only for a select few and not all men.

In the later chapters of this book, we will look at different ways you can get more than nudges but deeper insights and answers to the deposits and intentions of God for your life. We will also check out different tests that will help you discover them quickly as built on the foundation of connecting to the Creator from your Spirit. Building up the discoveries of our inner abilities upon this knowledge is paramount for long term stability in whatever area of life our purpose (life) and career or occupation is based upon.

Digging deeper is the way you think intentionally: What did I just do there? Why do I speak this way? Why do I analyse things like this? Why do I look at people from this lens of kindness or curiosity or inquisitiveness? Why, What, How, Why and Why again.

That said, it is pertinent to note that everyone is born to be purposeful. Not just to exist; but to live in purpose with a grand style in your chosen field of work – career, occupation, job - whatever it is for you. There is something for you, an area of impact that is specific to you, even you!

The Creator's first instruction to the prototype of man He created in Adam and Eve was to be fruitful and multiply, then He gave them a garden to tend to. The garden was *their* thing. You might say they had to leave the garden eventually due to their misconduct but then, there was something else for them which they left for. There is definitely something for everyone. A job to do, an occupation to follow, a home to tend to, people to help, manage or lead and even follow, and most importantly, a purpose to fulfil in all of these areas.

There is something for every single person to do, including you, that was designed intentionally by God. Let go of self-pity, hopelessness, and confusion. Your case is not hopeless. What you need is to search for and discover what it is that your Creator has made you for and what He has made for you.

The Two-Way Rule

There is a two-way rule to recognizing our God deposits and I call it the two-way rule because it works both ways. Even though the ways are different, they are aimed at a singular purpose which is, activating a deep-seated hunger and desire that was wired in us. They are rules because we need to pay attention to them.

These two rules should only come after getting your spirit connection in place, and they are:

1. Pay attention to what gets you compassionate for a good cause.

2. Pay attention to what gets you angry in a good way.

I will refer to these two rules as passion as I go on and I'll stress the good in both points because there are lots of causes that are not ultimately for good reasons. There are selfish, wicked and obscene causes people fight for all in the name of passion, religion or anger, but there is nothing good in them.

There is definitely something for everyone. A job to do, an occupation to follow, a home to tend to, people to help, manage or lead and even follow, and most importantly, a purpose to fulfil in all of these areas.

Our two rules, however, are the purest forms of passion and anger that stem from a good place of making positive and progressive changes in life, all to the praise and glory of God. This in itself fills every human purposefully.

These are facts that shouldn't be ignored or neglected. We should be aware and clear on this as everything we do and become would be more important based on the deepest intentions of the heart and where our purpose is rooted in. In other words, know your why, and if your why doesn't bring glory, praise and honour to the only true God who created you and gave you hope through Jesus, then it's not from Him. That right there is the rule of the two-way rule!

One way you will know you are in line with your Creator's blueprint is when it is evident that what you do is good, it is not outside of God's Word and it is in accordance to the measure of God's grace upon you and His deposits in you. It is good because everything He does is good. In Genesis chapter 1 verses 4, 12 and 25 and 31, God talked about everything He made and specifically stated that it was good. *"God looked over everything he had made; it was so good, so very good! It was evening, it was morning— Day Six." Genesis 1:31 MSG.*

Good in God's way and in God's eyes, which is good according to His Word and instructions in the Bible, is how you know that your passion is for the right cause and it is for God's agenda.

Know your why, and if your why doesn't bring glory, praise and honour to the only true God who created you and gave you hope through Jesus, then it's not from Him.

Another way to prove these rules is that they keep tugging at your heart, stirring up a divine hunger to become who we need to be in order to birth these longings in our best forms. Also, the divine hunger to do the work it takes to bring forth the fruits of our divine deposits.

The good kind of anger here is one geared toward a positive action for a positive cause. There must be actions and reflections that have stirred up deep empathy and compassion for people within you in the past. This is the time to start taking note of them and digging deeper like we learned earlier.

When you hear or read about a thing that puts a burden on you to do good, find a solution, remedy a case, stretch out a hand of help and comfort or encourage the people involved; these desires are not ordinary and you know so because your first thought is not about the benefit the action has to offer you or the good it will do for you.

Sometimes, you are exposed to something that spurs an emotional reaction from you; you get teary not just out of pity, but for the fact that you want to help the people involved and do something positive. By reflecting deeply, you can discover that you have what it takes to offer the assistance that is needed in these situations. You will have it in you, the deposits we talked about. These are the signs that help unveil to you everything God has placed within you.

It is extremely important, however, to always go back to God in prayers to be led on what actions to take about these desires as hasty responses never do much or lasting good. Remember that you can misinterpret these desires if you do not have that connection with God and you might even miss out on the right action to take. Let's look at the example of Edward.

Edward has these strong empathic feelings for singles who have experienced relationship breakups leading to heartbreaks and emotional trauma. He literally feels their pain. Now, Edward happens to be a successful architect who enjoys his job because it makes him happy and it pays his bills; he is quite financially buoyant and appears to have no worries. However, Edward cannot help but feel extremely discouraged and unhappy whenever he gets news about singles who go through emotional meltdowns from breakups. After a big break at work, Edward hears about his colleague who had a breakup episode and was filled with the same compassion so he assumed that by being there for his colleague who is a lady, he would feel better and so he began a friendship relationship with her. They ended up falling in love or so they thought and got married after some months.

Two years down the line, Edward discovers that he married his colleague out of pity and not from compatibility or divine leading; in fact, there was no chemistry as well. What he assumed was love was the same compassion he still has for other people in a similar situation, like he had for her initially; but he still doesn't know how best to respond, be of help or be a solution.

After realising this and reading the *Purpose Pathfinder*, he took out time to really know His

Creator and have a relationship with Him. Then he built himself up by studying the Bible which is a manual God graciously made available to guide us and more. He also got himself a professional Life Coach to navigate this trying season of his life and launch into clarity and purposeful living. This is when Edward realized that his experience and constant desire to help people going through heartbreak was not a problem or a curse that could keep getting him in trouble but was in fact a God-deposit he has for emotional healing. He gained clarity and started to pursue his purpose with more wisdom, starting with organizing a one-month mind-shift makeover bootcamp for young men and women who have suffered emotional breakdowns from breakups. He ended up in the right path, fulfilling his purpose and God's vision for him and also found healing and restoration for his marriage by God's mercy!

Not everyone gets happy endings like the Edward scenario I painted above and this is why it is so important to start by getting it right, then get better at fulfilling purpose.

Imagine how that experience was for Edward. Would you rather be him or focus on getting it right now? It is either we misunderstand our feelings or we end up misinterpreting it if we are not in a relationship with God. A relationship with God is what makes it easy to know His thoughts for us as our Creator.

Often, what we love to do or enjoy doing, differs from what we are equipped for and called to do. We can see this from the example of Edward above who was a successful career man. What he was doing was what he was meant to do and was good at, but that wasn't all; there was something much bigger than that and it was birthed later. We could say the emotional healing ministry and mind-shift makeover were his calling and he was fulfilling purpose on both levels. We'll dive deeper into the calling aspect shortly.

In concluding this chapter, pay attention to the two-way rule and their rule, as well as false passion and the misinterpretation of it. It is easy for people struggling at a venture to realise if they are or are not on the right path and if that is what they should be doing. But a person who feels seemingly fulfilled might find it more difficult to pay attention to his God-deposits.

Although this sense of fulfilment comes for all doing one thing or the other, it does not last long for those who have much more to accomplish in life than they currently are. Fulfilment and true satisfaction only stand the test of time if it is on the right path.

Now, I'm not saying that getting in line with God's design for you and delivering values borne out of your God-deposits would be an entirely easy road without any hurdles. What I mean is, instead of feeling stressed and unhappy, what you will feel is stretched and fulfilled despite the

A relationship with God is what makes it easy to know His thoughts for us as our Creator.

workload involved. You do not necessarily struggle in the purpose path, especially when you have a wisdom and strength strategy in place.

Like a hard drive exposed to more than needed and necessary, human desires and passions get corrupted every time from the external factors we expose ourselves to and the impact they make on our spirits. In the case of the hard drive, it would need to be formatted or scanned to remove the compromised content. So also, humans need a form of cleansing and renewal to pick the right signals to live and work according to the manufacturer's standard.

Your God-deposits are from within you, not from outside. Some passions might not be from God's deposits in you; these are false passions. If you would take your time to keenly observe, these are propelled by external factors you relate with daily and the desires that come from them. Desires for wealth, power, fame and so on, which are not evil in themselves, but are sometimes from a wrong motive. Desires to please someone, propel someone or prove a point to someone or to yourself, also birth these false passions.

When your motivation and course of life are carved from these external factors, it could take you far from living according to the Creator's purpose and even take you a while to realise it. From the outside, you may appear to be doing well and

When your motivation and course of life are carved from these external factors, it could take you far from living according to the Creator's purpose and even take you a while to realise it.

excelling, but deep down, there is no joy, and you derive no feeling of fulfilment or satisfaction from what you do. So, again, it is not about the benefits you have from your job or the happiness you get from your charity because happiness is timebound and does not always translate to true fulfilment. It is rather about doing what you are meant to be doing and deriving a sense of fulfilment and wholeness from doing it.

<u>Purpose Action</u>

Ask yourself these questions:

1.   Is what I currently devote my time and life to from the God deposits within me or from external factors?

2.   Have I interpreted my passion correctly?

3.   Am I truly satisfied and fulfilled doing what I do? Have I found soulful rest or am I still trying to get it right?

Be sure to honestly answer these questions.

CHAPTER SIX

KNOWING YOUR CALLING

Your calling, which essentially is another pathway to purpose, is the deep hunger we all have to do something specifically to satisfy the spiritual aspects of our being; and trust me, everyone is spiritual even if they don't know it yet. Your calling would be your spiritual consecration to the assignments you already have. The hunger and thirst to solve a problem using your God-given deposits.

Everyone who has been renewed into the God system and who can now identify God as her Creator, automatically has two callings in life: a spiritual calling to the salvation of men through the workings of God and ministry gifts, and a vocational calling to contribute to the cycle of life and make the world a better place.

These two types of callings are separate from each other but work hand in hand. The first one informs the way you will need to live out your second calling. The realization of what Christ has done for us produces a desire and longing to live for Him in a manner that pleases Him.

When I talk about 'calling' in this segment, I am speaking about the vocational kind that answers the question: "I know and have a relationship with God, but how does He want me to use my gifts and passions in the workplace?"

Your calling would be your spiritual consecration to the assignments you already have.

To begin with, asking the right questions is crucial for discerning your calling; again, in this sense, knowing your why is always major to success. Oftentimes, we do not ask the right questions and then we wonder why our answers are so dissatisfying. Seeking God's will for your life starts by asking yourself two simple questions:

1. What keeps me awake when I should be fast asleep at night?

   This is a question of vision and vision is what maintains purpose in your calling. The answer will expose what you can actually do for God and this informs the solution you have to give to the world.

2. What is the first set of thoughts that come to me when I awake to meditate each morning?

   This second question, similar to the first, informs your calling and the answer to this will uncover what you value, what you are committed to, what excites you in life and what is most important to you in life.

Consider these other relevant questions that are useful for deciphering God's design of you and His calling for you:

- What are your natural, God deposited passions and gifts? At the intersection of these two elements, you'll find your purpose in life.

- What would you work on or want to do for free? That is usually a good sign of what

God has designed you to do.

- What energized you when you were a child? Do those things still inspire you? Knowing your calling is often directly connected to your childhood passions and gifts.

- If you could do anything without any restrictions, who would you be?

- If you had access to any amount of money you need, what would you do with it?

From your answers to the questions above, what have you discovered? What are the barriers that are currently preventing you from pursuing your true calling? How can you begin to remove these obstacles?

If you aren't engaging your gifts and talents where you currently are right now, could you make changes in your current role to better engage them?

Finally, do not rule out the possibility that where you are right now is where God needs you to be and you can pick things up from right there; it is never too late.

Purpose Action

1. Take note of and take the time to find answers to all the questions that were asked in this chapter.

PART THREE

PURPOSE
PATHFINDER

CHAPTER SEVEN

PURPOSE IN PROGRESS

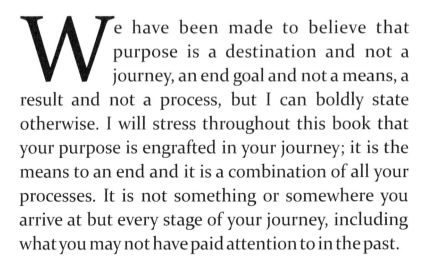

We have been made to believe that purpose is a destination and not a journey, an end goal and not a means, a result and not a process, but I can boldly state otherwise. I will stress throughout this book that your purpose is engrafted in your journey; it is the means to an end and it is a combination of all your processes. It is not something or somewhere you arrive at but every stage of your journey, including what you may not have paid attention to in the past.

In her book, *Hello Tomorrow*, Dr Cindy Trimm rightly stated that 'where your passion collides with the problems you see around you, is where you'll find your purpose.' Since purpose is found everywhere your passion brings the solution to a problem, consciously or not, then purpose is already exhibited in all these areas of your life. The keyword there is 'anywhere' so don't

> *Your purpose is engrafted in your journey; it is the means to an end and it is a combination of all your processes.*

think it is in just one area of life that your purpose can be manifested. It is in understanding where you ought to be per time and what you ought to be doing, that you find your way forward and discover your true desires, direction, destiny and destination.

We have had an in-depth look into identity and with the information we have gathered, it is important to be aware that everything and everyone God has made is fulfilling a purpose at every moment and everywhere. If you are currently in a job that you don't like and are ready to leave anytime soon, you have fulfilled a purpose there as it is not possible to be alive without achieving any particular purpose, be it the right or wrong one. It is now your choice to be at the right side of purpose, as the wrong side could mean you aiding an anti-god system, and I believe you don't want to be on the side which opposes your Creator. The Bible has succinctly equated this to life and death, and we are advised to choose life.

When there is any level of connection in focused prayers between you and your Maker, there would be an alarm that rings in your conscience, bringing to your knowledge what your purpose is in accordance with His specific design for you. It will also help you realise if the place that you are at any moment is where you ought to be or not. It is your responsibility to catch this and get necessary help to transition to the right path. If for any reason you are convinced that where you are is where you should be but still feel this tussle in your spirit and senses, then you need to identify what the root cause is, still in communicating with God.

It is in understanding where you ought to be per time and what you ought to be doing, that you find your way forward and discover your true desires, direction, destiny and destination.

An important aspect of living purposefully is to be intentional in all you do. Being intentional has helped me in my responses to life. If you experience any negative feeling at all: any little anger, anxiousness or envy towards someone or something, the first thing to do is to trace the source. Give yourself some good talk because it is very important to understand why you feel, think and act the way you do at every moment.

The law of purpose in progress is that purpose is not just a passing action or only for a particular point in time, it is in every breath and step. It is the entire chronicle of your life and what can be made of it. It does not last a season; the progressiveness of purpose makes it last our entire lifetime!

Purpose will continuously be revealed to you in stages so you don't need to be anxious or bothered about crossing it off your list like an action or an itinerary. You, however, should be concerned about the way you live your life at every moment because purpose is in a continuous stage, both in your conscious and subconscious states of living. Be deliberate about what season of life you are in, what you do per time, and why you do it.

This consciousness and intentionality begin with paying attention to your feelings. God put them there for a reason bigger than what it is averagely used for. Mastering your emotions and feelings are the first way to mastering being intentional in life as feelings often cloud our judgement. Even the strong, bold and decisive feelings are still emotions.

Emotions are fleeting, they do not hang around for long, they keep changing and might not be reliable in every case especially when they are based solely on the needs of the flesh – what you only experience physically and emotionally. The way you do life and the decisions you make should never be based on feelings until you have conquered your emotions as a tool from God, for Him to communicate with you.

Emotions can totally infringe on your actions and choices; they can determine the course of your life. Make up your mind on the feelings you allow to daily characterise your life. Let love, hope, peace, joy, forgiveness, and optimism characterise your life and colour your days intentionally. This is how to gain the clarity needed to boost your quality of life and fulfilment of purpose via intentionality.

The law of purpose in progress is that purpose is not just a passing action or only for a particular point in time, it is in every breath and step.

This is a self-mastery system that also

boosts the quality of your listening and understanding by improving on your levels of curiosity and awareness. This does not translate to being overly critical of yourself or overly self-conscious in a condemning or condescending manner, but simply being aware of what runs through your mind, what comes out of your mouth and the way you act. These are all factors that make your purpose in progress aligned to God's blueprint.

You can be self-aware without being judgemental; just keep to mindfulness and you will know the trajectory of your life and the ways you can make necessary changes. *Be like an external observer who is conscious of the way they are living their lives moment by moment, day in day out!* As the Bible puts it in Psalm 90:12 – *"So teach us to number our days, that we may apply our hearts unto wisdom."*

The changes you need for living intentionally might not be attributes you can develop in a day, but you can certainly condition your mind and your brain to begin to adopt this transformational process. You wouldn't know what transformation you need to be correctly aligned into the image your identity should ideally look like without the conscious habit of self-awareness. This would lead you to personal development actions that will guide you through the positive changes directed inward and reflected outward, to help navigate your purpose pathway.

With this understanding, you can discern what you are experiencing at the progressive stage of your purpose, if it is a struggle or a stretching. That's not to say there won't be any struggle on the right path you should be in, rather, to always remember that struggles only come to play when you've not found out the right ways of doing things that work for you. On the other hand, stretching might appear to be stressful when it's a new territory for you but you will easily adapt and adjust to the right condition.

Mastering your emotions and feelings are the first way to mastering being intentional in life as feelings often cloud our judgement.

If you are still trying to get a grasp of how to become more intentional about living out purpose, I pray you wake up to self-awareness, you find the right procedures, and you discover who and what to pattern your process after for the maximization of your purpose potentials, in the name of Jesus.

The reason you began this journey by understanding your identity, is so that you know you have been marked for a life of impact, purpose and destiny. In the light of these, it is important to note that there is no idle time in life. Every time you spend outside of a job or in waiting for the next stage of life, is an opportunity for more self-discovery and personal development that would help shape the kind of future that awaits you.

Purpose Action

1. Take a careful look at your journey so far in life. What are the intentional actions that have birthed purposeful results for you? Note them down and note down how you can become more self-aware about the actions that led to them.

Be thankful for your discovery.

CHAPTER EIGHT

PURPOSE AS A PROCESS

Now that you understand purpose to be a progressive action, you should also understand that it comes as little assignments, daily tasks, divine instructions from God and the people of God, and the simple but important obligations you have to fulfil daily. These are the step-by-step processes that comprise of purpose. These processes are series of actions that come alongside the various stages of your life. These assignments are not 'little' as it were, rather, they are the different aspects that are connected to create the true experience of satisfaction. These actions will confirm the fact that your life is aligned in purpose to God's intention for you.

In taking the simple, daily but life-changing actions as stated above, accuracy is something you must pay as much attention to as possible. In living purposefully, which can only be made possible when we understand the mind of God concerning the purpose He had planned out for us as individuals, we will, by design, have to take the step-by-step process approach.

While accuracy, especially in the things of God, remains a controversial topic among those who don't believe entirely in it, I can tell you with certainty that when you have complete trust in God and His leadership model for you, it leads you into accuracy in your process that you can't get any other way. Trust here is not the blind trust of following other people without understanding how they are led, neither is it a claim to follow God without a definitive relationship with Him. It must be defined so you know if you are following according to process or not.

Trust can be formed by following closely after God and following after the people whom you are sure are led by God and are right for your season of life. An example of a definitive trust process in God's leadership for my life is how He leads me through

His Word, through the Holy Spirit, and through my husband who again leads me by His Word. With this process in place, I am confident about what I am supposed to do per time, and I find it easy to resist any doubts that surface in my purpose journey. This following of God must be **closely, attentively and actively**.

Trust from following this process, constantly and consistently, is the trust that births accuracy. Pay attention to the keywords here - you have to keep to your **process consistently by following closely, attentively and actively** and you have to be **committed** to your **followership**. This way, your process will get clearer to you with time.

When you discover your process, learn to trust the process. This trust can't be taught but can only be caught by following closely after God and the people He leads you to.

Trust comes from a build-up of results. You can directly have access to accuracy from your trust process. It is like a tap opened to you, a knowing, a leading and a direction. Even when you don't know it, the hands of God, the voice of the Holy Spirit and that of your teachers, gently nudges you in the right direction; and years down the line, you will discover every path, every step, every twist and turn in your journey all through the way, is God's design for you in accuracy - when you commit to following as He leads you.

At this point, the Spirit of God now gives you access to the mind of God which seems impossible but is not. The scripture below has created a template to make it possible - by being in tune with the Spirit of God who knows all things, including the mind of God; and the Spirit communicates this with our spirits which our minds eventually receive.

> 1 Corinthians 2:16 AMP - *"For who has known the mind and purposes of the Lord, so as to instruct Him? But we have the mind of Christ {to be guided by His thoughts and purposes}."*

The second aspect necessary to be in tune with getting directions from God, is keeping our minds in a condition whereby it is able to receive from God. One very important thing we should take note of in our journey in purpose is that what we do, how we live or what we become, does not have to be like that of others. **In this journey of purpose, you are permitted to be different.** In fact, you were created to be uniquely different by the standards of creation. Looking back to how humans were created, though in the same image of God and likeness of one another, the creation process and their uniqueness is different.

Just as each person is made with a unique and individual blueprint by God, what success is to another person will be different from what it is to you. Knowing this will help you make informed decisions if you attempt to compare your process and journey in life to that of others. It will also condition your mindset, perspective and the permission you give yourself to be who God made you to be. **Failing** to understand this would make every other person's success look like it should be yours and you might end up being miserable in life, lacking contentment at the different stages of purpose that you should be enjoying. It can also keep you tied down, wasting time doing what you have no business doing.

> *In this journey of purpose, you are permitted to be different.*

As we have established earlier, knowing your identity and being aware of your God deposits, are not the only ways to have a good grasp of purpose. These two are the first and most important steps. The next step on what purpose, with precision, would mean to an individual, is the direction you get by receiving instructions from God and in being connected to His spirit. God's Spirit at work within you would imprint His directions upon your mind.

The Scripture from 1 Corinthians 2:16. AMP explains this concept of the Spirit communication better: *"For who has known the mind and purposes of the Lord, so as to instruct Him? But we have the mind of Christ {to be guided by His thoughts and purposes}."*

The key phrase here is, **to be guided**. Edward, from our previous story, had to connect with His Creator and engage in fellowshipping with Him before he could receive within his mind what he had to do; and this was how the bootcamp program was birthed alongside the destinies that were saved and reshaped.

There are lots of activities that appear to us like purposeful steps, actions, and decisions, when in the true sense, they are not. Meanwhile, God has all the answers ready at every step of life, so much that you cannot afford to get it wrong and you won't, when you are connected to Him. There is a reason we say He knows the end from the beginning. You might be unsure of your steps and footing on the paths of purpose but

If man-made navigation systems rarely fail, especially when you follow the instructions and directions correctly, how much more will God's direct leading get you to your destination? It's always a sure deal!

you will never be misdirected when you allow for His leading. It is like following the instructions on a map or a manual exactly as it is; you are never sure you'll get the destination right or get your desired effect but then you turn the last corner and find that you are finally where you are supposed to get to and you find what you want directly in front of you. If man-made navigation systems rarely fail, especially when you follow the instructions and directions correctly, how much more will God's direct leading get you to your destination? It's always a sure deal!

While some indicators of purpose will be related to and be in line with our talents and natural abilities, some would only appear like it because they satisfy different aspects of our lives except for the one aspect where we should experience the real satisfaction - in our hearts. These have similar expressions as purpose but are not purpose actions in themselves, and they could come from the place of compassion and holy anger therefore, fulfilling all the conditions possible for true purpose but it's actually a misdirection.

Purpose Action

1. Write out a list of directives you believe you received that led you into God's intended purpose for certain areas of your life.

2. In another note, list out those that turned out as wrong choices in the end.

3. Figure out the steps you took differently to get the different results you got.

CHAPTER NINE

PERFECTION OF PURPOSE

The worship of our Creator, love for and service to other creations, is the heart of spirituality and the encompassing components that perfects our purpose.

The secrets in this section will show you why you may feel you are on the right track and doing the right things but don't yet have a conviction that you are fulfilling purpose. This brings us to another two-way rule to get you to the point of restful assurance in your pathway to purpose. This two-way rule is embedded in the components that make up purpose, without which there is no complete satisfaction in the purpose pathway and they are: **worship, love** and **work**.

Worship is an integral part of our core as humans such that there will be a void within one's soul when such a person does not have a way to channel his worship or know how to do so. Same applies to when worship is channelled the wrong way or is directed to the wrong object.

> *The worship of our Creator, love for and service to other creations, is the heart of spirituality and the encompassing components that perfects our purpose.*

The general intent for which we walk the path of purpose is to find true satisfaction and total wellbeing for life, according to the way God has specifically designed our lives to be. To experience this true satisfaction, you must grasp the expressions that fulfil the conditions for a perfectly purposeful lifestyle and this spans across Worship of God and Love as a motivation.

1. **Worship of your Creator** – This is your ability to actively and thoughtfully appear, consciously and constantly, before the presence of God in awe, with appreciation, and in adoration. Rev. Olusola Areogun, an

ardent teacher of God's word, has emphasized worship as a manner of appearing before the presence of a deity. The only one worthy of our attention in this manner is the one true God that created all and He is our point of reference in this book. As much as spirituality is integral to well-being, we have to channel our spirituality in the right direction.

Worship should be your personalised way of loving up on God. Find time to study more about the actions and heart of worship and do this often, incorporating the 3 A's which are **Appreciation**, **Awe** and **Adoration**. Ensure they are channelled in the right direction and you will be surprised how your confidence and sense of fulfilment will rise immediately. Man was made to worship! Bear in mind that true worship is preceded by a correct recognition of and revelation of whom it is directed to. You have to see whom you worship as who He really is, to worship right.

2. **L o v e   a s   y o u r motivation** – Just as purpose is the reason and intent of your

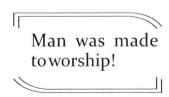

Man was made to worship!

existence, love should be the intent of your service. For life and for all things which revolve around your service to God and humanity, love is important to meet the requirements that qualify for perfection of purpose. It must be the basis of your commitment to God, and it must be your motivation to serve humanity.

Love in relation to your service will be your way of giving back to the community that raised you and the world at large, and this does an incredible job of filling your heart with a sense of purpose and fulfilment. Love would guide you into being a blessing to those who cannot pay you back for your service. It is pure love when service is done without the expectation of an incentive. The reward for your service does not necessarily have to be monetary; the joy and peace that come from it is an example. There is no fulfilment of purpose outside of love as we are created by a God who is love and wired to love. This love will spur in you the compassion and righteous anger to see that solutions are provided to the pressing needs of the community and expressions you have been called to serve.

3. **Work as the core** - Your work is a core part of the purpose path. Work in this sense could be slightly different from your career job but equally important in that it is what you devote your life to doing and is entirely based on the God deposits and divine abilities in you. Adam, the first man in creation, had a close fellowship and relationship with God which revolved around love, worship, and work. He had the work God called Him to do, empowered him for and blessed him from. *"And the LORD God took the man, and put him into the garden of Eden to dress it and to keep it."* Genesis 2:15, KJV

Your work would typically cover your career or profession, as well as your service from purpose. While your career involves what you were raised and trained to do, your purpose work will involve what you are divinely gifted for.

Work for me had always been split into two: my IT profession and my Coaching practice. Long before I knew what profession or practice I would be involved in, I exhibited the graces and had been going through trainings, studies, processes and examinations that would refine me in these areas, albeit unconsciously.

I have jokingly said, with some elements of truth, that I might have been a Life Coach from the womb. I've always had this innate ability to explain, advise, instruct, lead and help others, sometimes gently and sometimes fiercely; being a first child also contributed to this. I found out much later why these attributes come easily to me. The way my professional certification came about and how I have been led into this work, have all been evidences of the leadings of God.

My work is purposeful for several reasons, most important being that while I am not motivated by the reward, yet it comes. I could stay at it for hours and thoroughly enjoy every moment of it. It is as though time ceases to exist when I'm on coaching appointments and I smile as I type this. Work is indeed the core of purpose and it is pure bliss when you are in the right path.

The empty feeling of purposelessness ends at the point where a person completely understands the scope of purpose and the seasons of his life. This is why a person can still feel under-fulfilled despite all they do.

> *Work is indeed the core of purpose and it is pure bliss when you are in the right path.*

In the pathway to purpose, love for God and fellowship with Him comes first; and when these two factors are in place, the space in your heart to become more and to do more gradually becomes more meaningfully occupied with a dependency on God and a satisfaction from Him. You also gain clarity on the progressive steps to purpose in your life.

Some things we turn to, to fill the void in our hearts, only do a temporary job. For instance, things like charity would fill some space in your soul, and your paid job would dominate your mental capacity and your mind; however, the real deal is in having a spirit that finds contentment and true satisfaction only in God.

It is this worship and love that fills your heart. Your work and calling will keep your spirit contented because via relating with God's Spirit, your spirit will guide you to do both of these according to His will (Amen).

As it reveals a lot about the one doing the work, your work will expose your underlying character, motivations, skills, abilities, and personality traits. As the Bible puts it in Ecclesiastes 9:10, *whatever your hand finds to do* – should naturally be what God has equipped you for first, and it should be gotten from His directive, motivated by love and for His good cause - doing this with all your might will become a reward for you, not just an effort!

Good practice is to not stick with what you are not equipped for or to do what you don't have the ability to grow better at after you have read this book. We all have a freewill to choose what to do and how to use the special gifts God has given to each of us. We find peace and joy in work when we do it to bring glory to God and help others; and it brings Him glory when we are not only efficient but excellent in what we do.

Let me mention again with emphasis that no purpose is insignificant, too small or too massive for you. Purpose is unquantifiable and it is never only for a specified amount of time. The plan is till eternity!

Purpose Action

1. If you don't already have one, set up a worship routine you will keep to and follow the notes in this chapter with a pure heart to worship frequently.

2. What are the changes you can notice in you, starting from your first session?

CHAPTER TEN

PATHWAYS TO PURPOSE

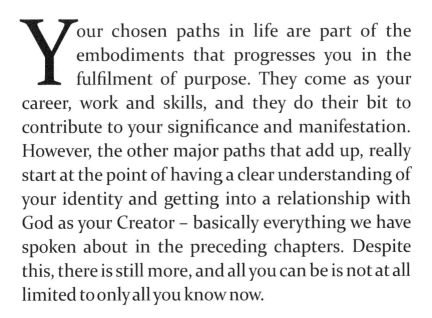

Your chosen paths in life are part of the embodiments that progresses you in the fulfilment of purpose. They come as your career, work and skills, and they do their bit to contribute to your significance and manifestation. However, the other major paths that add up, really start at the point of having a clear understanding of your identity and getting into a relationship with God as your Creator – basically everything we have spoken about in the preceding chapters. Despite this, there is still more, and all you can be is not at all limited to only all you know now.

According to Proverbs 4:18. AMP, *"But the path of the just (righteous) is like the light of dawn, that shines brighter and brighter until [it reaches its full strength and glory in] the perfect day."* This is the path of the purposefully led life, it keeps shining till perfection.

Asides your evident skills, there are still treasures within you that might not be obvious to the other humans around you or even to you at the moment. But when you do the job of digging deeper and bringing these out, they will take you to places you never imagined you could go.

When I was starting out my career journey with applying for a course in the university, the bandwagon effect and the realities around me affected my choice so much that I chose to be a science student in high school simply because that was what my intelligent classmates did. Although I had a natural flair for literature, I didn't pursue this. That flair comes in today in my creative writing, content creation and other sides of me that aid my core purpose.

I wanted to study Microbiology in the university but I was rather admitted to study Information and Communication Science, a course that has thankfully, remained relevant in changing times and with global developments. Niching down in my IT career, I was not certain what to do but my husband was instrumental in guiding me through the right career choice, navigating through the vision I have for myself in my career journey. Every path in my purpose journey has been discoveries and orchestrations carefully crafted out by God and uniquely designed for me. I have gone through processes I didn't understand fully at the beginning and then seen how it aligns to my future and purpose down the lane.

You must be in sync with God to see His purpose for you play out beautifully for He is genuinely interested in you living purposefully.

God alone knows your true capacity and capability and can give you what you can handle in the unforeseeable future. Let's look at the example of David. He was only a shepherd at the beginning of his story but turned out to become one of the greatest historical Kings. Through his journey, he was a musician, a warrior, was under siege at some point and generally went through extremely turbulent times. He ended as the King of his Nation with a special book of praise and was called a man after God's heart because he walked closely with

You must be in sync with God to see His purpose for you play out beautifully for He is genuinely interested in you living purposefully.

God and obviously put his best efforts in all he did – what a truly fulfilling life!

There is so much more to you than you currently know of and purpose will encapsulate all of your divine expressions into one magnificent story. Never be intimidated by where you are at the moment. No matter how daunting the future looks, know that you can and will get there. Only begin with the right vision and know that smallness or nothingness is not what God has in mind for your future even if that characterises your beginning. It is okay to start small. What you look like and how things currently seem, are not limitations because God is awesome at creating great things from absolute nothingness, making the little you have to be of great significance. It will all add up in the end.

It is not God's intention that we live a random lifestyle without intentionality; so, you can be confident that every path that has led you to where you currently are, have done their bit in propelling you towards the right path and the better way. The plan of God for us is always according to His specific intention and design which is easy to navigate when we are walking with Him. With your will and permission, you can easily navigate into the pathways He has divinely orchestrated for you. This is a real thing!

When you miss out on certain paths on your journey to purpose, there will always be grace to get back in line and it is never too late to do the necessary work to get back in line. Knowing now that you are designed and saved specifically to do the works God has called you to which is - the good works specifically required of you – you are obligated to do them.

One thought you must never nurture is *you don't know what to do* because not knowing what to do is not a thing. You either know it or you will know it. You won't know it all at once, no one does; but as for what you need to do at every passing time, you will know it by the leading of God's Spirit in you.

In *The Search for Significance*, Robert McGee notes that "As Christians, our fulfilment in this life depends not on our skills to avoid life's problems, but rather on our ability to apply God's specific solutions to our problems."

There is no fun in encountering twists and turns in life when you don't know what to make of the disruptions that happen to you. Making sense of these disruptions doesn't have to go the conventional, natural and painful way of figuring things out on your own; or the tests and trials method. There is a simplified, proven and accurate way of correcting your steps via the wisdom of God. You need the correct understanding and interpretation of your process to be able to trust the process. This is when you can see God's intended purpose for your experiences and receive God's specific solutions for you. The only way to access these is through a relationship with Jesus as the only link to God.

Never be intimidated by where you are at the moment.

The journey into your purpose is not one you should take alone. A community of like-minded believers and a community that catalyses your vision, will go a long way in helping you stay on the path of purpose.

God who knew you before you were born already made you to start showcasing your gifts as a child and has embedded the signs into the details and junctions of your life which will be visible to significant people in your life. Who you are and whom you would become, are fashioned into your DNA so you can be sure you have been unconsciously walking with the trails of purpose on every track you have gone through, in every footstep you have taken and on every pathway you have passed. In Christ, these realities become clear to you and you can be saved from paths that do not align to God's plans for you.

CHAPTER ELEVEN

PURPOSE CATALYSTS AND PURPOSE DISTRACTIONS

To live purposefully is entirely your decision, COMING THROUGH what you choose to allow and what you choose to disallow. One of the first questions I ask during my coaching sessions revolve around knowing what the most important thing for an individual to achieve at every moment is. And this is something everyone should know for themselves and strive to get done.

Purpose is like that big thing but it is not just for a moment. As a continuous journey, it is of utmost importance, more than the other big things we always have in every season. Living purposefully is the most important thing after getting into a relationship with God, yet it is not that much sought after. Living purposefully is attainable in different areas of life. It is possible for a person to feel purposeful in one area and feel like they are failing in another.

While the previous sections on mastering your emotion and the perfection of purpose are very valid and should be mastered to become well-rounded and successful according to the standards and definition God has ordained for you, mastering this will be dependent on understanding your purpose catalysts and the distractions we will be looking into below.

My first question for you in this chapter is: what spurs you on to living in line with God's purpose for you and what deters you from that path? I will ask this again at the end of this chapter so you can take a while to think about it now and we will get back to it.

Purpose Distractions

Whenever a person is involved in something that looks good to the world and is acceptable according to the standards society has set for it, such a person appears to be fruitful because of the 'good works'. However, when we are determined to live purposefully according to the standards and the pathway that God as our Father has set for us, we understand that everything that appears good is not necessary God's design for us. While everything that is from God is good, not everything that is good is necessarily from God. How to adjust our mindset such that we can focus on the things that really matter, is by recognising what the good, purposeful work and life for us really means and getting together the factors that keep us fixated on these alone without swaying from the right path.

The bulk of things we engage in will either propel us or take out from the actual time we need to do the things that really matter to our destiny. Things that take us away from the purpose paths are purpose distractions.

Not everything that is good is needful; some are just distractions. A question you can always ask yourself is, if everything you engage in per time is profitable for you individually. How are you spending your time? Now is the time to stop getting distracted by the unnecessary good, and solely focus on the needful and important.

The world of technology and the society have presented us with so much we can expound our time on – the time, technology and manpower that can be focused on doing the truly relevant things to living purposefully. For some, this is not even the distraction, rather, other good things that become overused or misused, like sleep and leisure time. These in themselves cannot be underestimated; it only becomes a problem when it takes from the time you need to do other things that are more relevant to you. The same way some other productive activities could be less significant to your specific, unique journey.

I love the Biblical example we have of Elisha who at a point in his life (after he was already very successful at his work) discovered that the purpose path and calling for him was to follow Elijah and take over from him as a Prophet. In doing this, he could have decided to keep his work as an extensive agriculturist, but he knew this would be a distraction for him. Two things he understood were: he now knew what the real thing was for him, and he knew when to retire from the previous thing. So, he threw a retirement party for himself, shared out or we can say, invested his accumulated wealth in his community as this was needed for him to face the next step of his life without any distraction.

This realisation can happen for anyone at any point in life which is why it is never too early or too late to start walking the path of purpose. The entirety of your life would have prepared you for this in the first place. For Elisha, it hit him at the point he already had an established career and already carved a life around it for himself - he already had a great life and living, and was already wealthy and famous. But he did not hesitate to leave it all behind to focus on the journey ahead of him; he was wise enough to end that business intentionally, and forge ahead on his life's purpose.

To think you've gone too far on a path to take the right turn means you've not gotten to the place of highest desire or to the lowest point of discontentment. The only thing these feelings should do for you is propel you into getting answers. Determination that comes from knowing what truly matters to us in life and destiny, and the pursuit of this, will lead us to the right choices in life.

Do you already know that thing that matters most in your life? Are you ready to let go of what you're currently building to face that squarely?

The good things that side-track us from the purpose pathway today can be: side jobs, career pursuits, ministerial assignments you were not divinely led into, leisure, fun, play, extended rest time that leads to laziness and lack of responsibility. It could even be the clubs and societies you belong to, or the social activities you dedicate every weekend and the most energetic moments of your life to. Your distractions could also be the friends you hang out with, or the company you keep.

Determination that comes from knowing what truly matters to us in life and destiny, and the pursuit of this, will lead us to the right choices in life.

It is time to look into what to cut out entirely, for those you can do without, and reduce those you can spend less time on or with, gradually taking charge of your life again. The time you spend engaging in every other thing will significantly impact your purpose. There is always a balance and this comes with wisdom. It comes by delegating your time wisely.

Wisely dedicate your time to work, you should also dedicate time to recharge and re-energise yourself. The recharge time is the best time where you unload and reload from God's Spirit for what lies ahead of you.

Purpose Catalysts

Purpose catalysts, on the other hand, are those activities that spur you on, closing the steps you have to purpose. They are the seemingly little assignments which really count and bring about the changes that matter.

These catalysts might not come up as urgent a lot of time, but they are always the important things and they matter the most. They might appear to you in subtle and sublime things, but they are the weighty choices that push your life in the right direction. A twist to purpose catalysts is that they might take a significant amount of your time and not be the real thing, but they heavily prepare and energize you for the real thing.

Let's look at a general example on preparation. For instance, if you need to get a physical job done, like cutting down a tree, and you spend more than half the time sharpening your axe - no machinery, as this paints a clearer picture. Or say, you have to do a presentation and you spend days preparing your slides and points for a 30-minute presentation. These preparations are catalysts. Never handle these with any amount of levity or triviality.

For some, it's the job they do; they excel at it by putting in the effort and this success propels them into worshipping God with more awe in their private life and God reveals greater secrets to them for dominion at their work place and ministerial assignments which helps them gain more grounds purpose-wise.

All these actions speed up the action of purposeful living. Take your purpose catalysts seriously!

Purpose Action

1. Create a list for yourself, stating your purpose distractions and your purpose catalysts.

It is important that as you begin to complete this book, you constantly think back on what we have covered so far that has led to this point. Engage in the activities mindfully, take the extra mile today and engage the discipline of focus. *A single eyed focus on your unique and specific journey as ordained by God, is the only way you can get to your destination in life.*

PART FOUR

PURPOSE
REFLECTIONS

I n this concluding part, we would go through some exercises – Interpersonal and Intrapersonal, with practical steps that will take you through the journey of understanding your abilities and graces, and which will be relevant to your professional or vocational purpose pathway. You will find the relevance of this section applicable to any purpose pathway you choose.

Your reflections consist of, but are not limited to, how you have been perceived by people who are closest and dearest to you, how you see yourself, how God sees you and the derived beliefs that you have allowed to shape your life from these different perspectives. Remember, the last two perspectives are what matters most - yours and God's. The people in your life can only give their perspective based on how they have observed you, but this doesn't make them entirely right – it is only to give some perspective to you.

These reflections are indicators of your inner abilities from your portrayed outlooks. They are defined by the way you think, act and speak as your truest self without the conditioning from external factors. They point at your God deposits. They are series of discussions you need to have with yourself and with the people whom you know truly love you and who know you in your realest and truest form. They are questions you need to ask to revive the innocent expressions you had as a child. These expressions are mostly original to your personality but might have been lost or mismanaged in the process of growing up and the experiences you have had such as criticism, human judgements and the likes.

These reflections are something you want to talk about and re-consider.

CHAPTER TWELVE

ABILITIES AND GRACES

"There is no ordinary person, everyone is robed with dignity from heaven and designed to flourish in life when they walk in their unique, specific graces."

L et's begin with shinning some light on your abilities and how they can be different from your graces. While these are similar, they can be confused for each other. Anyone can be whatever they choose to be; this is what abilities can make happen for different people. That said, it is a dangerous adventure to choose to do a thing only because you have the ability to do it. A person who is determined to walk the path of purpose with an accuracy of the Creator's blueprint in focal view, must be one who inquires, clarifies, and is led into all he engages in.

Grace, on the other hand, is what you naturally would not have the ability to do or talent for, but which you supernaturally are able to carry out; and it rides on the wings of work. You will be able to easily distinguish that the things you do or achieve are not merely by your power or as a result of your intellect, but something more; and you are right. Grace will insert beauty and distinction to your work strategy and it is so important as it is what differentiates you from others. This grace is only accessible when you are on the right path God designed for you.

Purpose is an embodiment of abilities and graces in you for what God has prepared for you. Nothing is a mere coincidence, or a matter of luck for a person who has a relationship with God. Your purpose path happens by specific, intricate designs and ordinations from God. Yes, God may use humans to show you this but it is not a human arrangement.

Taking time to consciously reflect on your abilities and graces will bring you into an understanding of how God has led you, and a glimpse into where He is leading you to. This will then inform your

> *Purpose is an embodiment of abilities and graces in you for what God has prepared for you.*

immediate decisions and your futuristic, lifelong choices.

Applying the supernatural force of grace to what you already have ability for, will give you the power that can generate for you the capacity to do phenomenal exploits in the areas that have become clear to you.

Friends, I want you to know that grace is real and it works when you make it work! This entire book is a work of grace; literally following the flow of the Spirit in creating this project from start to finish and trusting in His wisdom, especially on days I had no idea what to type. But as soon as I conditioned my mind to work the work, the words begin to flow until I stop again. So yes, grace is a thing.

I will emphasize again that grace only works when we put it to work. The muscular nature of the brain makes it such that it can grow; it is resilient and can take in any information, developing creative results with the data it is presented with. Again, when we put it to work.

Your ability is not all there is to you, when you utilize grace, you have much more. Grace, sometimes, does not need an existing ability as it can create this for you and even recreate lost abilities. Certain

> Your purpose path happens by specific, intricate designs and ordinations from God.

capacities that are beyond abilities are only given and made available by God's grace and your yielding to the work that comes with this grace.

Amazingly, everyone has a measure of grace and with work, you can make this grace grow. God has given you the needed amount of ability for your career path which is why it is important to be aware of the actual grace and enablement you have for a vocation before getting into it. After this, you would now determine if you can work this ability much more into a skillset that produces a ripple effect of successful outcomes.

A lack of reflection on your graces and abilities will eventually lead to continual burnout causing frustration, discouragement, and depression. To avoid this, there is wisdom to understand and engage the systems that empower us for a journey of purposeful living such as coaching, mentoring and the right communities.

Your ability, in terms of your gifts and resources, is something you must be attentive to in order to have an understanding of what you can achieve. Know what you can potentially achieve, then put it to work.

There are cases where you might have desires for a particular solution to a problem but not have the specific ability to provide the answers directly. In such cases, you could choose to get into a partnership whereby you resourcefully get the answers and gain the knowledge you need while actively contributing towards your source in return. An example of this is volunteering. In this same vein, you also need people who can see the abilities in you. While you look more using your own eyes, you should be willing to see as well from other people's view and perspectives, especially those who are dear to you and sincere with you.

These reflections will have to go through a timeframe of the past and the present for more accurate interpretations as the growth and seasons of life come with differences and changes in personality. The most important traits that define your abilities would however, come mostly from your childhood. To complete the exercises, you will have to dig up a lot of old memories and reconnect with the right people.

CHAPTER THIRTEEN

INTER AND INTRA REFLECTIONS

"Your reflections are a culmination of your interpersonal and intrapersonal views from your past, present and future ideas and actions."

Interpersonal Reflections

This is the relationships you have had and continue to have with other people in the communities and environments you have been around that has shaped you in one way or the other. This starts with the first interactions you had as a child. You might not remember most of the things that happened at this stage, but you have people who do. It might take a long-distance phone call or a visit to your previous home and place of birth to find out more details about yourself.

Ask your parents or guardians some questions or go through old documents and report cards – the type you get from nursery schools describing your nature in the classroom and around school as observed by your first set of teachers. You will be surprised at the treasures you find and how this can help in defining your immediate future.

Dig deeper again, like in the previous section, but this time, dig with your first community. You might need to talk to older siblings or childhood friends who remember certain things you might have forgotten. Note that this does not have to be all formal; take it as a vacation and have some fun while investigating for your purpose pathfinder.

Dig up old time memories in a fun, interesting way: it could be a lovely visit or a friendly phone call. You can organise a hang out, go camping, hiking or host a dinner. Anything to juggle your memory. Most importantly, do all of these with the help of the Holy Spirit who always knows much more than anyone else.

As you unveil your discoveries, record it all in your journal or have your device handy to keep track, ensuring you don't miss out anything helpful or important. The first stage will likely start with your parents, nannies or guardians; people present around your birth and growing up stage.

Let me add that in doing this, you would do very well to keep track for your child(ren) if you have any. Make a conscious effort to record the important stages and details of their lives. When they grow up and you present this to them, it would be a priceless gift and you would have kickstarted a purposeful lifestyle for them. I see focus and concentration in my daughter since when she was a baby. How she goes, "no, I'm working", whenever she's busy with something and you try to break her focus – it's so sweet and deep at the same time. These and many other attributes like this are worth noting for your children to help them understand their strengths and learn to work around this in the future as they learn to walk with God.

Also, it is important to gain the insights of your colleagues, your superiors, and your subordinates. If you do a 9–5-hour shift working 5 days a week and physically too, you probably spend most of your time with these people. That does not mean you have to gauge or measure yourself by their opinions; this is simply to note their opinions and dig deeper by comparing your past traits with your present actions.

Compare your successes. What has changed around your abilities and capabilities, the way you perceive it and the way others do? Then determine how you would make the most of this information.

Intrapersonal Reflections

These are what you have discovered personally from how you relate within yourself using your mindfulness. It entails what you have discovered for yourself from understanding your identity and inheritance as God's Creation and Sonship in Him, in conjunction with what you have discovered for yourself as a conscious learner who constantly looks inwards. Remember, no one can know you as much as you know yourself, asides the One who made you.

This stage is where you take out some personal time to retreat with yourself and think back, comparing personal notes. Allow your thoughts to go back to the plans you've had for yourself in the past. If you kept these in journals, you can get them out and start going over them again. Think about all the things you wanted to do, those you have done, those you haven't done and what really stopped you then; everything you ever cared for and was concerned about, then carefully consider the two questions below:

A. Are those passions still alive in you? Is there any flicker of hope alive for the desires?

B. Are the abilities, strengths, and skillset required for those passions still available? If not, do you have the grace and capacity to invest in it and are you willing to do the work required?

You need to be as honest as possible with your answers here. You could reach out to the people closest to you at present to investigate this with you and ask for their honest opinions. Remember, with the intrapersonal, we are currently dealing with personal interactions from the past. Time has gone by, your strength, focus and responsibilities are probably all different right now but be honest with yourself with where you currently are in your journey (progressive purpose), using this information for your purpose as a process for the end goal of accuracy and ultimately, sustainability.

The Role Of Core Values

Your intrapersonal reflections would not be complete without the powerful role of core values in giving definition to your essence in life. There are dangerous cycles you could fall back into in life if you live life without the mindfulness of your core values. To ensure and enforce this mindfulness, is majorly by cultivating a values evaluation activity for yourself. I would advise this to be done after you have had one professionally and now know how to get it done rightly.

If you have never had a core value session, this is something you may want to invest in and you can do this by investing in a form of coaching that would help you wholistically in discovering where you need to be, what you need to be doing, how to get there and how to get it done by yourself.

In my career coaching packages, I have established a model I call the **career-identity matrix system**. This is a structure that replaces limiting beliefs with lifting ones, establishes intentionality and lifelong learning practices using the relevant model, and completes the process with a curriculum on realignment of purpose.

The point here is that in your coaching experience, you will get to that point where you need to identify your core values and your coach will guide you through this exercise professionally. Your core values give you a stand point perspective to what your life is about and how the activities around your day-to-day life, especially if you are interested in living purposefully, comes in to give a definition to why you do things the way you do them and how you can intelligently and intentionally improve on your actions. It goes without saying that this ultimately improves your lifestyle!

A simple guide to identifying your core values is to look at different aspects of your life - I like to segment this into spiritual, moral, education, financial and other aspects of life and pick a word that describes what is the most important thing to you in each of these areas as it concerns your life.

Your core values go a long way in showing you first-hand if you are living authentically and being who you say you are - especially in the light of the knowledge and understanding you have gained from this book. To get the most from core values, I like to suggest to my clients and I can also tell you freely that you need to consciously review your values at least bi-annually. From my discoveries, it is proven that reviewing your core values constantly helps you reflect on the current state of your values and to discover what has changed in the past months. This conscious understanding of what have changed, especially after reading a book like this one, will help you realise and manage more effectively the degree at which you are living authentically and purposefully.

Personality Tests

Your reflections are not limited to the interpersonal and intrapersonal only; you can find out more using technology for profiling. Before that, it is important to un-condition our minds from how the society has profiled living purposefully or responsibly. Perhaps, why you don't know what you are graced for or haven't discovered your strengths and abilities, is because you have no idea of the possibilities available to you and the strengths you are endowed with.

Many have been conditioned to only believe that being well versed in literacy and numeracy skills or excelling in the arts and business, is all there is to living purposefully and successfully in life. Society has sold a lie to people and some parents and guardians have even affirmed this lie, making innocent millennials and Gen Zs to believe that an inability to be skilful in some areas of life or skilfulness in handiwork and creatives such as planning and organizing, or arts and crafts, or wood or metal work, or beautification or cooking skills or even street-sense, is a limiting factor which makes a person a defective commodity in the community.

While all these are life skills to have which cannot be faulted or discouraged, I want you to know that you can still be alright with having, honing, and maximizing just one or two of these skills, and be able to afford a life that allows for everything else. All you need to make it in life is already in you; anything you decide to add should be that - an additional skill, not what would make you.

It is okay to not be a jack of all trades; only aspire and invest into being a master of one or more.

There are different versions of the lies that have been sold to you, but your job is to stop believing those lies and start believing the truth because only the truth can make you free and confident enough to be who God has called you to be, using what you have already. You will be surprised at what exists outside the universe you have been conditioned in. If you would like to know more, you can explore the two powerful and very helpful options I will share with you here. The first, you might have heard of or done before, or you could have even tried both. However, that should not

It is okay to not be a jack of all trades; only aspire and invest into being a master of one or more.

stop you from doing it again, more intentionally now.

The first is the DISC test for professional skills, and the second is the Gallup strengths test.

- DISC test (online)

- Gallup test (online)

The goal is to keep discovering yourself, keep evolving, keep getting it right and continue to get better.

Evolve

In concluding this chapter on reflections, let's talk about how you can evolve into something better and more beautiful from what you have discovered about yourself. One thing I discovered from my upbringing and the society I grew up in, was that a lot of people in their lifetime forgo trying out new things. Only a few people really go all out. A lot of people think basic skills and activities like swimming or touring are luxuries for a privileged few.

You don't have to go to the deep-end of something you have not tried before, but you can always begin to explore and discover new possibilities in you that you never knew existed. Exploring your intellectual and bodily strengths help you have a grasp of your abilities. I mentioned earlier the muscular nature of the brain; the way we exercise our brains is the same way we can exercise it for new skills, new methods of doing things, and new routines and helpful habits. Train your mind and body to maximize your graces and abilities by putting in the work necessary for the change you want to see.

It is not enough to discover your purpose pathways in life, you need to dig deeper and stay in fellowship to continually receive from God the accuracy for your progressive purpose. What matters most is that you stay consistent at it; that is the way to have true satisfaction.

To experience the perfection of purpose, you need to stay consistent with worship and maintain a heart motivated by love in your workspace. Let this be the foundation of your work. The Bible tells us in 1 Corinthians 3:21. GNT, *"No one, then, should boast about what human beings can do. Actually, everything belongs to you."* All things are yours and so whatever you fail at is nobody's fault but yours alone. With God on your side, you literally have all that you need by His Spirit's leading, and the wisdom from this book, to live in purpose daily! God has explicitly provided all you need to come to your fullest potentials, and I truly hope and pray that you permit yourself to expand your abilities and harness your graces. Go the extra mile in righteousness today.

Trying out new things would require a lot of courage and boldness that God has already empowered you with. All you need to do is make the bold moves. Get past your comfort zone, try out new, exciting adventures, study on investments to grow your wealth, put yourself out there, look for volunteering opportunities in the areas you should be making a difference in, invest your time in developing your skills and talent. Do not be a local champion, extend your tentacles beyond your horizon! Also, discover new strengths by trying out new things. Don't miss out on adventures you can be potentially awesome at because you never sought for an opportunity to try. A lot of talents will never be discovered, let yours be among the few that will be discovered and harnessed.

There are new games you can attempt to build your aptitude and workplace productivity. When you set a timeframe to it and ensure you don't get carried away, making it a habit to practice this often can be a rewarding activity. For example, you can download *Elevate* and give the game a try using the various learning areas to increase your capability while having fun. You can also engage in board games that enhance your linguistic, logical and mental abilities like Scrabble, Sudoku and Chess. Try out sporting activities you're not familiar with, even if you are not a sports person.

> *To experience the perfection of purpose, you need to stay consistent with worship and maintain a heart motivated by love in your workspace.*

I know this sounds wild but this is not only to keep you fit and maintain your bodily vessel; you never know, you could become a world champion from just starting out that sport you have always had a passion for! No Kidding! Consider music, some painting, etc. I challenge you to learn and do something new and see how this enhances your life and choices.

Begin to discover for yourself what the possibilities of your talents and giftings are, and in what activities they might be hidden. A gifting for a particular activity could be a pointer to a similar one that requires the strength you possess in that area. You can refer to the chapter on recognizing your God deposits for how to wisely navigate your interests, calling and strengths around your purpose paths. Evolve!

CHAPTER FOURTEEN

PERSONAL MASTERY

Going forward with the understanding of and realisation of purpose, a lot is hinged on what you can receive and perceive about yourself accurately, and this is already well discussed in the previous chapters. In this penultimate chapter, I will be sharing some specific steps to help you discover more about yourself, what you should be doing in relation to what you have found out and examples of what you need to discover in order to get the results you would like to achieve, sooner, after doing the due diligence of following every step and process.

At this stage, if you have followed well, completed the purpose actions and activities in the previous sections (which I trust that you have), you would already have a good grasp of your purpose, and it is already carved around your values and personality even if that wasn't clear to you at first.

Question 1: What stage am I at right now in defining my purpose and living it out? What am I doing NOW?

Question 2: What do I need to go forward? What am I to do NEXT?

To move forward from a specific point, you need to realise where exactly you are and then learn how to go forward. You can answer these questions on NOW and NEXT by defining all your present and past achievements. As Curly Martins, Author and Life Coaching Expert puts it: *"when you know your life's purpose, it is easier to make the right decisions when making life defining choices."* This means defining your purpose from an understanding of who you are makes your big decisions and your steps in life easy and confident choices.

How you define your purpose is from the understanding of what you have discovered from your identity, your passions and strongest convictions, and your calling as revealed to you with accuracy from your relationship with God. Since we have established that purpose is a lifelong process that is bigger than you, you will realise as you journey through life that your purpose per time will always resonate around what you have learnt about yourself. All of the above is what defines your purpose – specific to you, and this is why you must understand your journey in and through life. With what you have discovered and your definition of purpose, you can easily discover where you currently are in fulfilling it.

Defining your purpose from an under-standing of who you are makes your big decisions and your steps in life easy and confident choices.

Addressing the question of knowing what is next and what to do to go forward, is the point where you must take actual steps towards decision making. Opportunities will always abound, and doors will be open occasionally, but it is your decision to know which opportunity to take and which door you need to step into. You might not be a hundred percent sure about your next move but it is important to always know what you need and what is most important to you in life by revelation. This will define your next moves. Let me add here, very importantly, that clarity and conviction are two things you can never afford to live without. You will always remain where you are till you know where you are and what you need to do next. Make a decision to start something from what you have been reading here and start somewhere, somehow. Sometimes, it is in the process of starting something that you find the real thing you really need.

A bonus question for you here is: "What stands me out?"

We've talked about our uniqueness in this book and this is the point where you practically list out everything that stands you out from others. This is the point of checking and balancing your authenticity, and the stage where you ensure you're living life in your natural self, not forcing anything and not making yourself into who you are not, while evolving in your God-given strengths and abilities.

I will share here an example of a big decision I made recently which required me to first answer the two questions above. I had just relocated to the United Kingdom and needed a career change but I wasn't sure what to go into. So, I kept applying for various jobs that looked like what I could do which was going to pay me, and I got quite some offers. However, for some reason, I couldn't quite bring myself into settling into any of those jobs.

Carity and conviction are two things you can never afford to live without.

Now, I already knew about myself, I knew where I was at, had a good grasp of my sense of purpose and my peculiarity to a great extent, but I simply couldn't figure out how to move forward. In the meantime, I volunteered and worked almost full time while searching for a fixed job. I worked as a volunteer with a coaching organisation and another non-governmental charity organisation for Africans in Diaspora and I was working virtually at both capacities with amazing people around the world. While this gave me a great sense of fulfilment, I knew I had to start at that season something that would be relevant to my strongest passions and would be original to me.

In spending quality time with God, everything began to come together. Meanwhile, I have been following the principles I put together in this book for a while. Consequently, I received my next step and knew what I had to do - I knew how to go forward immediately and was convinced about what to do next. It was an opportunity to train for a skill I naturally had the ability and grace for, and it also involved me investing into becoming a professional in that area and that was how *Nova Results Coaching* was birthed.

The good thing is that when you begin to align with purpose, everything else that could potentially limit or hinder you, will begin to give way. Somehow, my volunteering engagements were completed around that same season without me planning that out initially, and I completed this professional training in half the required time. That was me easily stepping into a life-defining choice because I already knew my life's purpose. You can do the same with the knowledge in this book.

So, where are you right now and what are you to do next?

The next stage for you might be understanding your identity; for someone else, it could be understanding their God deposits; for some other person, it could be to dig deeper or know their calling; and for some others, it could be to understand their abilities and graces or to hone their skills for vocational excellence.

I was conscious of where I was at the moment and what I needed to go forward. This made me see clearly and not miss the opportunity to take the steps when the opportunity came along. This will be a recurring process that takes us all higher in destiny and I pray we never miss out on any moment in Jesus' name.

CHAPTER FIFTEEN

DESTINY CAN NEVER BE DENIED

This final chapter is an encourager for you, my dear reader. Destiny is the manifestation of the purposes and intents of God upon a man's life. The key word here being **manifestation**, which is everything that you have embodied, revealed to you in stages. Nothing could ever stop that. This is a decade of destiny, and it is a chance for fulfilment of prophecy when you begin to step into purpose.

> *Destiny is the manifestation of the purposes and intents of God upon a man's life.*

Destiny cannot be denied for a person who has accepted Jesus to be Lord and Saviour to them and have submitted to the leadership of the Holy Spirit.

Nothing could ever stop you from destiny even if it tried, the only limiting factor would be you if you fold your hands and do nothing. You are in the process of manifesting God's purpose if you start out right and continue better.

Destiny could go the wrong way if you fail to get it right.

When we talk about destiny, it is important to come out of the past and thoughts of the time you have lost. Destiny has a way of catching up with people when they finally get it right. Time lost may not be regained but there will always be a chance for you. You have not lost a thing when it is all restored back to you; God is a restorer.

> *Destiny cannot be denied for a person who has accepted Jesus to be Lord and Saviour to them and have submitted to the leadership of the Holy Spirit.*

Life is in stages and destiny happens for you at every twist and turn of it. This is not something that happens to you, it happens in you, through you and

> *Destiny could go the wrong way if you fail to get it right.*

for you! That is destiny and it will never put you in the position of a victim but that of a victor, if you allow it.

Having read all the way to this point, you cannot possibly go back to doing life as usual. There is something knowledge does to you which makes the difference.

When you begin to see things from the fresh perspective of destiny, you begin to ravel in the joy and strength to become more. Please, do not go back to the wrong mindsets. Remember, destiny is happening *for* you right now and it will continue to happen for you positively.

> *Destiny is happening for you right now and it will continue to happen for you positively.*

FINAL WORDS

We have discussed extensively throughout this book the four pointers to purpose which are: *vision, encounter, calling and revelation.* I was concluding the last section without realising these pointers when the Holy Spirit dropped it in my heart. These points are the summary of everything we have discussed in this book. You can review this again alongside this book and hold them dear to your heart. Let these points remind you of all the stages involved in living purposefully.

Vision is the foundation of **Identity which is** Your ability to see yourself the way God sees you. **Encounter** is understanding your **Sonship** and

recognizing the Creator as God and discovering His deposits in you. Calling is your ticket to the **process of purpose**, and **Revelation** is the perception of and **perfection of purpose**.

Don't ever stop at any point and do note that it doesn't end with the last point because vision started this and vision never dies. When the Bible talks about the path of the righteous - who you are now if you have started on a journey with God, according to Proverbs 4:18 - it was talking about vision. As your path shines brighter, your vision gets clearer. You hone, sharpen, and clarify repeatedly as you journey through life.

Revelation births worship and there is no fulfilment outside of worship. We are wired to look up to God to find higher purpose and to be reliant on the bigger force.

Finally, I have emphasized throughout this book the importance of answering the questions and completing every activity. It will make me very glad if you do this; and for yourself, the impact will be massive. There is a reward system I use personally which has helped me make something out of everything I invest in. This reward system is to

achieve something from everything I pay for or have invested my time or energy in. You should make something massive out of this and feel free to share your encounters, testimonies and mind-shifts from this book with me on:
purposepathfinder@novarcoaching.co.uk

For your life and career coaching enquiries, you can send your enquiries to:
faithehira@novarcoaching.co.uk

Thank you so much and continue to live in purpose daily!

THE END

ABOUT THE AUTHOR

FAITH EHIRA is an amazing, influential and balanced woman who lives in purpose daily and spreads the fragrance of Christ everywhere.

She describes her purpose journey as one borne out of an accurate understanding of her identity from the Creator as well as her God deposits, with a drive to leverage these into being a blessing to the world. She is productive, progressive and profitable from executing her passions, with God at the centre of it, and with a community of like-minded, values aligned believers; and she loves to influence others to do likewise.

Faith is called and equipped to share the great importance of purpose to fulfilment in a person's life. She is a Certified Practitioner of Life Coaching and specializes in purpose coaching for life and workplace fulfilment. She works with individuals to discover the genius in them and achieve their big dreams by harnessing their unique strengths and innate values. She hosts *Purpose Conversations with Faith* on YouTube and a podcast series known as *The Anointed Series*.

Faith is happily married to David and they are blessed with children. She lives in the United Kingdom with her family.